Cross-Country Cycling

The Guide for the Off-Road Leisure Rider

Jim McGurn

and

Edgar Newton

Hodder & Stoughton

LONDON SYDNEY AUCKLAND

Photographs: Sue Darlow, Jason Patient, Mike Lomas,
Tony Annis, Paul Burrows, Jim McGurn.

Special thanks to Geoff Apps for his help and advice.

Ordnance Survey Landranger Sheet 94 Map of
Whitby (1989) reproduced with the permission
of the Controller Of Her Majesty's Stationery Office
© Crown Copyright.

Special thanks to Sustrans for permission
to reproduce 'The Cuckoo Trail'.

British Library Cataloguing in Publication Data

McGurn, James
Cross-Country Cycling: Guide for the
  Off-road Rider
I. Title   II. Apps, Geoff
796.6

ISBN 0-340-58654-0

Published by Hodder and Stoughton,
a division of Hodder and Stoughton Ltd,
Mill Road, Dunton Green, Sevenoaks, Kent TN13 2YA.
Editorial Office: 47 Bedford Square, London WC1B 3DP.

Photoset by Rowland Phototypesetting Ltd,
Bury St Edmunds, Suffolk

Designed by Behram Kapadia

Printed in Italy by
New Interlitho S.p.A., Milan

Contents

CHAPTER ONE

Taking to the Trails

Cycling on many trails and country paths can be a family affair.

Cycling off-road does not necessarily mean heading for the hills. Many cross-country routes are relatively undemanding.

The bicycle, mankind's most happy invention, has taken to the great off-road. Millions of cyclists are discovering the world of cross-country tracks and bridlepaths, on new generations of low-geared, lightweight off-road bikes.

The new off-roader is a touring cyclist, whether out for a day ride in the hills or a week-long off-road trek with panniers full of camping gear. This is green tourism at its best. Once it is apparent that off-road cycling can be a friendly, non-threatening pastime it will become even more attractive to beginners and existing road cyclists. Many more will realise that there is no compulsion to dress in gaudy Lycra or tear across the countryside with few thoughts in mind other than how to manoeuvre the bike past this or that obstacle without slowing down. Aggressive mountain biking is going nowhere. In the United States it has led to bike bans in many sensitive rural areas. So serious is this danger that the US mountain bike industry, mindful that bike bans mean lower cycle sales, is exhorting riders to show consideration to the environment and to others.

This book is therefore not about performance mountain biking, which is a young and distinct branch of cycling with its own set of attitudes, values and fashion statements. Instead it has been written for those who see the off-road bicycle as a delightful means to a delightful end, rather than as an end in itself. A well-equipped, reliable machine will bring you closer to the magic and magnificence of nature. You will get to where you want to be thanks to your own intelligence, skill and strength; and your safe, sensible riding techniques will ensure that you cause minimal soil erosion as you go.

To differentiate between the two cultures of cycling, we have generally used the terms mountain bike and mountain biking to mean the fashion-based pursuit which emphasises performance. We have used the terms ATB (All-Terrain Bicycle), off-road cycling and cross-country cycling to signify the broader, calmer approach. Of course, there are many cyclists who would position themselves somewhere in between the two extremes. There are also organised events which span both forms of cycling, requiring both physical prowess and powers of perception.

There is little to compare with the quiet thrill of an unhurried ride through wilderness, at a pace fast enough to take you an appreciable distance, with

Good cross-country cycling often entails some road riding first. Taking a quiet, wandering country road can be as much fun in its own way as riding on the rough.

varying vistas, yet slow enough to let you appreciate the nuances of nature. The exhilaration of off-road cycling goes hand in hand with the health and fitness benefits of this often demanding style of travel. You can ride off-road with great enjoyment without putting your body under much pressure. However, there is little sense of achievement if you do not exert yourself just a little.

Motor tourism, on the other hand, demotes the human body, seals you off from the environment you travel through, and causes its own environmental problems on the way. True, cyclists can get wet, but they also experience the best of the elements. You learn to watch the sky and understand its ever-changing patterns. At one time you'll enjoy a scented breeze, at another time you'll feel the kiss of the sun and occasionally, yes, it will rain. This book tells you how to cope with these elements which are, after all, part of life. Self-reliance can be fun.

You can ride almost any bike off-road. Jim McGurn has toured off-road in all weathers on a standard road touring bike. It was a bit bumpy at times but the bike never failed him. For decades the Rough-Stuff Fellowship has

been achieving some amazing off-road feats on sturdy versions of touring machines. Jim has even travelled short distances off-road on a child-carrying tricycle – an amazing experience involving much lurching and body-positioning, to the delight of the children on the back. Further back in history, American riders of the high wheel (now known as the penny-farthing) regularly practised off-road riding skills. Dutch cyclists, with their large 28-inch wheels, have no trouble coping with the gravelly paths and cobbles on many of their excellent cycle routes. Right across Africa and Asia heavy ungeared Raleigh roadster look-alikes are ridden on dirt tracks and unmetalled roads.

However, new and exciting technology is available in your local bike shop, at very reasonable prices. At last the British cycle industry is beginning to offer fully equipped ATBs suitable for touring. Cyclists in other European countries have had such bikes for decades. This new breed of bicycle, known as the hybrid or the town-and-trail, incorporates the best of mountain bike technology with the best design principles of the touring bike. The hybrid bicycle has yet to settle down to any recognised standard. design. Some

What's good for the trails may also be fine for the town. No bike need be a weekend wonder.

Getting closer to heaven in the Cheviots. Modern bicycle technology allows anyone reasonably fit to go further and higher than before.

remain little more than slightly redesigned mountain bikes. The fully equipped models mean that off-roaders no longer need to buy a bare-bones mountain bike and then spend about half as much again having touring accessories fitted. A good, well-equipped off-road bike will also be useful for riding around town, since city streets can make demands on the commuter cyclist which are not too far removed from the demands of the dirt track: both situations require an upright riding position with good all-round vision. They also both require manoeuvrability, sturdy wheels, powerful brakes, a rack for luggage, a wide range of easy-to-find gears, and a strong frame.

Whatever the bicycle, inexperienced buyers often find it difficult to distinguish between a low-quality machine which rides like a dog, and a reliable, high-spec bike which handles like a dream. They can sometimes look very similar. Even within the same quality bracket, you need to distinguish

between an ATB designed for touring, and one designed for out and out competition.

Just as a good modern off-road bicycle can make a big difference to your riding comfort and what you can achieve, the use of appropriate cycle clothing can make all the difference between exhilaration and discomfort.

In this book we give you the information you need to make the decisions which are right for you. We have supplemented our own knowledge by gathering together the experiences of a wide variety of off-road cyclists.

It does not take much to get touring on the trails: all you need is a good bicycle, some basic knowledge and an awareness of the need not to attempt too much too soon. It's fun out there and it's that rare form of fun which costs little, spares the environment and is good for the soul. Take to the trails!

Cycling and photography have been allied pursuits since Victorian days.

CHAPTER TWO

Choosing the Best Bike for You

Cyclists took off across the country on atrocious roads, for a century before the mountain bike was born.

Modern bicycles are excellent value. This is because large, competing manufacturers buy their components from all over the world, selling huge numbers of machines in order to keep the prices low. Most mid-range ATBs have perfectly respectable frames built in the Far East, with reputable components made by Japanese-owned companies. European manufacturers also produce a fine range of machines, often incorporating traditional frame-building skills.

This leads to a bewildering range for the first-time buyer to choose from. You need to ask yourself honestly what you will be using the bike for. Only then should you step into a cycle shop, where you will be dazzled by a pantheon of gleaming parakeet-coloured mounts with gung-ho names such as Stone-Breaker, Fat Track, Rough Trade, Die Hard and Timberline. Making the right choice in the first place will avoid expensive modifications later. Because manufacturers use their purchasing power to keep the price of their components down, it is much cheaper to buy a complete bike which will immediately meet most of your needs than it is to have your ideal parts retro-fitted.

If you want a bicycle for commuting to work or going into town for shopping or evening classes, you will need more than a basic ATB or one of the 'hybrids'. You will need mudguards, lights and probably a rack to carry panniers. These are items which the competitive cyclist would regard as unnecessary clutter, yet if he were a down-hill ace he might regard a pair of suspension forks costing at least £250 as essential kit. Saddles are another example of specialised componentry. The racer will rarely remain long in the saddle, which has therefore been reduced on competition bikes to a thin wedge, similar to a typical road-racing saddle. You will probably prefer a more sedate style, and look for a more supportive seat. If you choose a bike without the accessories you really want, make sure that they can still be attached: some competition models will not accommodate the fittings for fixtures such as racks and mudguards, nor have the clearance for them. If, for example, you intend to go touring, you might want a frame with mounting-holes for a stable four-point-fitting rear rack, and a couple of water bottle cages.

A downhill racer might relish this aluminium racing bike with front suspension and narrow saddle.

Despite the appearance of hybrid bikes in recent years, there is no bicycle which will serve every purpose equally well. Hybrids are essentially sturdy street bikes and are not designed for the extremes of cross-country use, although, with care, most will be fine.

If you're new to off-road riding, you could consider hiring a bike. This will give you an appreciation of how different sorts of bike feel. Hiring a bike (for £10 or so a day) might help you avoid some expensive mistakes and give you the confidence to shop around. You can also pick up many useful tips from a competent hire operator while they set the bike up for you. To find a local hire business look in the small ads of bicycle magazines or contact the Tourist Information Centre of any major touring region.

A well equipped hybrid – fine for many cross-country jaunts, although the mudguards will become choked in muddy conditions.

What is your bike to be used for? This kind of robust bike with panniers, mudguards and hub brakes, can be used off-road and in town.

While the cycle industry may be dominated by large manufacturers, real innovation in bicycle design has often been the work of enthusiastic individuals and amateurs. The mountain bike was born out of the passion of a small group of Americans for hurtling down rough tracks on modified old American roadster bikes. It quickly became apparent they could double their fun by building machines light enough and sufficiently well-geared to be ridden back up again. So the first mountain bikes emerged out of small workshops, to be rapidly copied and mass-produced by Far East manufacturers. The mountain bike has been rapidly modified during its short history. This is because adult bicycles have never before been subject to such widespread and joyful abuse. Design assumptions have been tested to the limit and many modifications made. Bicycle enthusiasts love novelty and many unusual steeds have appeared, to be discarded and forgotten after a short season.

Early mountain bikes incorporated many of the characteristics of their parent American roadsters. Traditional wisdom was that a comfortable roadster should have laid-back frame angles, giving a long wheelbase and easy and relaxed steering for that long limousine ride over road bumps. The laid-back frame and design might be fine for a lazy roadster or, in a less

You can now buy tandems which are rugged enough for off-road use. They need to be carefully designed, because the rear rider's pedals can ground on bumps which the front rider has already passed and can no longer see.

exaggerated form, for touring. The demands of mountain bike competition require a more compact and agile animal: more a mountain goat than an ox. Modern ATB design has followed the competitive trend, producing a machine that can, if the rider desires, dance nimbly over rapidly changing terrain and around unexpected obstacles. Strength has to be allied to lightness, giving rapid acceleration where conditions permit, or high power up punishing gradients with dreadful surfaces. To enable the driving rear wheel to grip under slippery conditions, it helps if the rider's weight is over the rear wheel. So, for example, the rear wheel of a competition bike is brought in nearer to the rider, making for a shorter wheelbase.

The modern ATB has many other features which distinguish it from its ancestors. The frame is smaller and generally has a sloping top tube which provides greater crotch clearance (or stand-over dimension) if the rider slips off the front of the saddle. The frame may be made of fatter tubes, because a tube with a bigger diameter and thinner walls is stiffer for the same weight. The bottom bracket holding the cranks is slightly higher than on a road bike for greater ground clearance. While most frames have the traditional diamond configuration (long recognised as the best arrangement for steel-tubed

Traditional frame built with good alloy steel tubes brazed into lugs. Note the Reynolds transfer near the steering column. The tyres on this model are chunkier than necessary for leisure off-road cycling.

bicycles) the increasing usage of other materials has led to frames featuring a wide variety of designs.

The frame is the most important consideration when choosing a bike. It will determine the overall feel of the bike, how lively it is to ride, and how resilient. Steel is the traditional stuff of bicycle manufacture and bikes designed for city and cross-country cycling will often have a high-tensile steel frame. For more expensive frames, manufacturers employ steel alloy tubing. This is a stronger material and therefore the tubing can be lighter. A commonly used steel alloy is chrome-molybdenum or Cro-Mo. Bicycles made from superior quality tubes always have labels proclaiming this virtue. Read the small print on the tubing label to see how much of the bicycle is constructed with the tubing you require.

Further weight can be saved by butting the tubes. This process thickens the tube ends where extra strength is needed for brazing them to the adjoining tubes, while thinning the centre section for lightness. Steel tubes are sometimes joined together by lugs, which are fixed by brazing. Many long-established manufacturers build their cross-country frames in this traditional manner (Dawes of Birmingham, for example) and claim that brazed lugs provide more strength than direct tube-to-tube joints, and a less brittle joint than welding, which requires higher temperatures. Raleigh, the best-known British manufacturer, has modified the lugging process by bonding the tubes to alloy lugs, avoiding the necessity of brazing which can sometimes weaken the metal in mass production. It also simplifies the joining of metals that would otherwise require difficult specialist techniques: titanium, for example, needs to be welded in a vacuum. However, bonding titanium tubes into alloy lugs has brought the price of titanium frames down from the stratosphere.

Aluminium is a frame material which has become increasingly popular in recent years. You will recognise aluminium frames by their tubby tubes,

wider because aluminium is not as strong as steel. They are welded together directly without using lugs. Manufacturers such as the Cannondale Corporation of America have refined aluminium frame production to provide excellent touring bikes as well as competition mountain bikes.

Carbon fibre has emerged as the wonderstuff for bicycle frames since such a mount propelled Chris Boardman to an Olympic gold medal. The designer of the frame, Mike Burrows, has been proclaiming its potential for years: 'It is the lightest, strongest and most versatile material you can build a bike from for racing bikes, for mountain bikes, for tourers and for shoppers.' This versatility lies in its ability to be moulded into a complete frame with no joints or even tubes. According to Burrows, from now on 'tube frames are dead'. The appearance of bicycles is likely to change faster in the closing years of the century than at any time since the first chain-driven bicycle was produced. Mould-pressed bikes will rapidly become cheaper as they go into mass production. However, carbon-fibre frames are still a long way off.

The introduction of the ATB was an immediate success with the public, and rapidly became the fashionable machine for city cycling.

Why this sudden success? One reason is that they look good with their bright, chunky styling. They are, above all, very practical and user-friendly. The novice feels comfortable on an ATB because of the more upright riding position, with the gear controls mounted on the handlebars near to the levers of relatively strong brakes. The ATB will feel more secure than a drop-handlebar touring bike (which traditionally has the gear levers

Moulton All Purpose folding bike, suitable for off-road recreational riding.

Town bike suitable for light off-road use. This de luxe roadster by Dawes has a five speed hub gear, and many lightweight alloy parts. More than anything, the alloy wheels help give a zippy performance.

mounted on the frame). The rider can concentrate on traffic conditions rather than keeping an eye on the road surface, because the strong wheel rims and fatter tyres can cope with the uneven surfaces of many poor urban roads.

Riders in big cities such as London came to realise that they could greatly increase the performance of their ATB by changing to slicker tyres. So if you plan to do a lot of city cycling, you might consider getting two sets of tyres to allow for different types of ride. Keeping your spare tyres on spare wheels means that change-over is fast and easy, thanks to quick release axles, which are now common.

Because ATBs were such a hit, manufacturers were keen to adopt many of their most attractive features for other types of bicycle. They also wanted to create a range of bicycles with larger, narrower wheels and tyres (and perhaps mudguards and racks) more suited to city use. This gave rise to the 'hybrid', a vague name for a catch-all category. Some of these are near-mountain bikes which can be used for any kind of riding; others have a frame much like a traditional roadster, with lightweight equipment.

If you live miles away from satisfactory country tracks or hilly country, or if you expect to ride off-road only occasionally as part of longer tours, you should consider purchasing a traditional touring bike. Cycle tourists began 'rough stuffing' a century before the birth of the ATB. They have been setting out on world tours over unmade tracks for just as long. Provided it is well-made and equipped, the only factor to consider is whether it will suit your needs and riding style. The drop handlebars of a traditional tourer are best suited for long journeys on the road. They offer up to four different hand positions, enabling you to vary your posture and to crouch down into a head-wind. The straight handlebars of ATBs allow no such variation of posture. This can be improved by the use of bar ends, which are short handlebar extensions rising up at right angles to the bars. Now some ATBs have handlebars swept forward like the horns of some creature of the veldt. However, you may prefer something in between.

It is vital that the bike you buy has a frame that is neither too large nor too small. The wrong size frame may force you into an uncomfortable riding position which will only become apparent once you begin riding in earnest. The easiest way to estimate the size you require for a traditional commuter or touring bike is to divide your height by three. However, ATBs often have a higher bottom bracket to give greater clearance when you're going over obstacles, which changes the frame size requirement. The size of frame to choose for an ATB is therefore somewhat smaller than that of a touring bike for the same rider. The test for a right-size frame is that you are able to straddle the bike with your feet flat on the ground and with at least two inches of clearance between your pubic bone and the top tube of the frame. Adjustments in saddle and handlebar height are dealt with in Chapter 3.

We are not going to describe in detail the virtues of different types of derailleur gears, chainsets and brakes as grounds for choosing one cross-country bicycle rather than another. This is because most bicycles of reliable

On a mountain bike, the rider is in a relatively upright position, with the gear levers mounted on the handlebars, near to the levers of relatively strong brakes.

Traditional touring bicycles with well built wheels are fine for many off-road tracks.

quality are equipped with these components made by one dominant manufacturer. Further up the price range – above £700 – there is greater variety. This reflects the specialist needs of the enthusiast and is beyond the scope of an introductory book such as this. You can easily spend over £2000 for a bike. However, do check that your bike has aluminium rather than steel wheel rims. Much of your effort goes into turning these revolving parts and you will get a livelier and more responsive ride if they are made of aluminium. Also, avoid bikes with cheap steel chainsets and cranks. There are a lot of so-called mountain bikes around. They may look chunky, but their colourful paint jobs can distract the eye from mediocre and inefficient components. Choose a good bike shop, tell them what you want a bike for, spend as much as you can afford and learn about cycle maintenance. Follow these rules and you'll have a good bike for life.

CHAPTER THREE

Modifications and Accessories

An important and recent development in saddle technology is the gel-filling. These saddles 'give' at the point of contact, whereas sprung saddles move and tilt as a whole. Leakage of gel is extremely rare.

Although it is best to buy a bike which meets as many of your immediate needs as possible without modification, there are some changes you can ask for at the time of purchase which will not add enormously to the price. There are also those changes you will probably wish to make after you have been riding the bike for a while to mould it to your character, style or riding position. You may, for example, want to alter the arrangement of the saddle and handlebars so that you gain the maximum benefit from your effort whilst in the most comfortable position. If the saddle is too low it will cramp your style and reduce your power. You may find yourself sliding over the back of your saddle in an unconscious attempt to stretch your legs, or your knees might start to ache from the strain of a restricted position. Place your heel on the pedal and raise the saddle until your leg is almost straight when the pedal is at its lowest point. (Take care to avoid raising it to the point where your pelvis rocks from side to side as you pedal along.) There is a more precise formula: measure your inside leg from crotch to the ground while barefooted. Multiply this measurement by 1.09 and this gives you the ideal distance from the top of the saddle to the top of the pedal at its lowest point. Check that you have left a safe length of the stem inside the seat tube and that the maximum extension mark is not visible once you have the saddle adjusted to a really comfortable height. If there is no maximum extension mark on the seat pin, leave at least 2½ inches of seat pin inside the seat tube. It is worth marking this position on the stem, perhaps with a piece of PVC tape so you can quickly find the right height again should you ever need to move it. To find the correct fore–aft position of your saddle, sit on the bike and put your foot on the pedal at the three o'clock position. Using a plumb line (which could be made from a bolt tied to a length of string), move the saddle until the knob on the side of your knee aligns with the centre of the pedal. Don't be afraid to experiment until you find the exact position for your leg, saddle and pedal combination.

Manufacturers may keep the price of a bike down by fitting an indifferent saddle because few people would consider saddle quality as a key feature in choosing a bike. Yet it is the seat which is the support for your cycling effort and a cheap one can cause persistent discomfort. When buying a new bike,

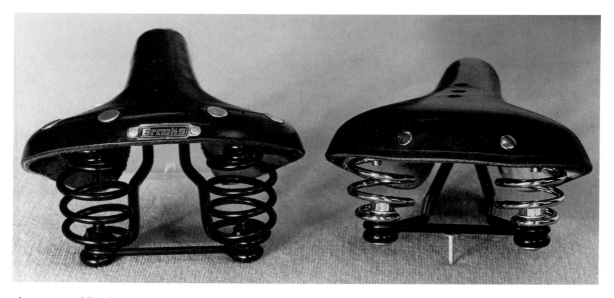

always consider buying a better saddle or fitting an old favourite. Saddles can be narrow or wide, hard, sprung or padded with gel, made from moulded plastic, leather or even carbon fibre. The best type for you will depend partly on your sex; women generally require a broader saddle than men. Your preferred riding position is also a factor; if you favour an upright position which will not spread your weight to the handlebars, you need more shock absorption in the seat. Brooks of England, Lepper of Holland and Ideale of France are all renowned for their leather saddles. These can be beautiful pieces of craftwork. The rich-coloured leather (sometimes secured with hand-

Sprung leather saddles by Brooks (left) and Lepper. Sprung saddles are not in fashion for mountain bikes, but can be a simple solution to soreness for longer distance touring off-roaders.

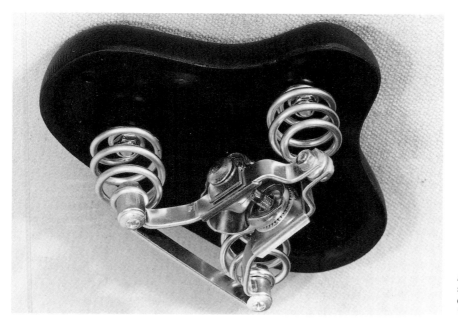

A well sprung and supportive saddle from Lepper. This design was around in the 1890s.

19

Above The serrated band around the handlebar stem shows the minimal insertion distance. It should never be visible when the stem is fitted. Once the height of the stem has been chosen, the stem is tightened into position by means of the allen key bolt which sits at the top of the stem. This forces upwards and outwards the wedge shown at the bottom of the stem.

beaten copper rivets) will mellow with age and use, lasting for years provided you dress the top with cream or oil occasionally. Brooks' saddles have a nose-tensioning bolt which takes up any stretch and prevents the top from eventually resembling a hammock.

Soft saddles may not necessarily be as comfortable as they appear because they may not provide adequate support for the work you are doing (you would not work at a desk in an easy chair). It may be better to dampen road shock with a sprung saddle instead. However, saddle padding materials have improved tremendously in recent years through the insertion of various elastomer gels.

Another major modification you might wish to make (at an acceptable price) is to change the handlebars and the stem which holds them in position. This is a fairly frequent alteration made by people who like classic touring bikes but not drop handlebars. Changing the handlebar shape will make a dramatic difference to your riding position and the way your weight is distributed. A simpler way of doing this would be to raise or lower the handlebar stem. This is more complicated with stems which have an integral brake cable stop because the front brake will have to be readjusted afterwards. Make sure if you do adjust the stem that the minimum insertion mark is

not visible. If this will not allow sufficient height for you, you may need to buy another stem. SR produce one which gives about 10 inches of height with minimal forward extension for an extremely upright position.

You can choose different styles of handlebar to modify your riding position. Straight, ATB-style handlebars can be uncomfortable on long road journeys because they tend to lock the elbows in one position, and for this reason you may prefer a more traditional, swept-back style. Inexpensive bar-ends can be added to mountain bike bars to offer a greater variety of riding positions. It is possible to construct all manner of arrangements for your handlebars. Jason Patient (who took some of the pictures for this book) favours inverted, sawn-off drop handlebars to give a more upright riding position, with three hand positions; and another colleague, Geoff Apps, has achieved a dignified 'Victorian' position by the use of a home-made stem and a forward positioned saddle. You might find a handlebar with a shallow drop which you can use either way up. Check when purchasing the new handlebars and control lever that they are the right diameter for your stem and control levers.

Suspension systems are very fashionable with mountain bikers and some can be retro-fitted, but there are disadvantages which can outweigh their usefulness. Cheap and badly adjusted suspension can cause the bike to rock

The fitting of a long Stump Neck stem allows a more upright riding position.

Opposite above right The Girvin Flexstem is a useful add-on component for riders with wrist problems.

Opposite Whatever takes your fancy . . . Jason Patient, who took many of these photographs, rides on- and off-road with inverted, sawn-off drop bars. The only criterion is personal comfort.

21

This cyclist has fitted bars with an upwards bend, which is useful for pulling against when hill climbing. Alternatively, bar ends can be fitted to existing straight handlebars. If this new hand position is adopted, it is wise to fit Dr Dew brake lever extensions, as shown.

Gel-filled cycling gloves help ease the pressure.

too much, absorbing energy that should be going into pedalling. Suspension systems are also quite complicated to maintain. Look first at simpler ways of improving the comfort of your ride by modifying the weight distribution, trying a sprung saddle or fitting more robust tyres which can be run at a lower pressure. One effective yet simple modern product that will increase shock absorption for a moderate price is the Girvin Flexstem. This is a handlebar stem which pivots against a polymer disc. It will absorb rapid, moderate vibration but cannot deal with big bumps. You can also cushion the handlebars with both shock-absorbing handlebar grips and the use of gel-padded gloves.

A more expensive and fundamental modification that you may consider is to convert to hub gears. Many people, confronted by a shopful of bicycles with twenty-one or more gears, wistfully recall the robust simplicity of those three-speed hub gears on their first bike. A few drops of oil and a very infrequent adjustment of gear cable tension would keep it running smoothly throughout the years. In contrast, modern derailleur gear systems give you a wonderful range of gears, and allow you to change gear while you continue to pedal, but they are exposed to dirt and water, easily bashed and require frequent adjustment and replacement of parts. Sturmey Archer produce a five-speed hub, refined over the years, with a range of gears wide enough for most cyclists. Sachs Huret also produce hub gears and brakes. However, with the dominance of derailleur gears, not all bicycle shops have the expertise to adapt bicycles to hub gears. Sturmey Archer have established a network of dealers competent to do so. (Contact Sturmey Archer on 0602 420800 for their list of LINK UK dealers.)

Unfortunately there are few quality bicycles, other than basic roadsters, available in Britain with hub brakes (Dawes and Pashley are exceptions).

Internal hub gears, by Sturmey Archer or Sachs, are ideal for gentle off-roading. The range of gears is limited (usually three or five), but they are virtually maintenance free, and unaffected by mud and the elements. These gears are not found on off-the-peg off-road bikes.

Conventional mountain bikes are fitted with a derailleur gear changing system. The spring-loaded gear arm extending below moves in and out, shifting the chain from one sprocket to another, on the block of different sized sprockets. The Shimano system pictured here incorporates an especially long gear changing arm, which is needed to allow the chain to reach up onto the 34-tooth largest sprocket. The bigger that largest sprocket, the lower the gear for hill-climbing. This derailleur system is complemented by another derailleur further forward, by the pedals. The front derailleur will have two or three chainwheels, which are the equivalent of the sprockets on the back. Gears are found by combining a choice of chainwheel at the front with a choice of sprocket at the back.

However, hub brakes make good sense in wet and muddy conditions for the same reasons as hub gears, and offer a smoother progressive braking action in all-weather conditions. Any cyclist who has pulled on the brakes in a downpour, with white knuckles, to get no response will appreciate the need for all-weather brakes!

It will seem unbelievable to many cyclists (especially those who have lurched into a roadside hedge after being dazzled by a motorist) that the power of their laughably feeble lamps is limited by law. The maximum output for cycle lamps is 3.6W (or 2.4W if halogen). You are allowed to use more powerful lights off the road and there are some high-powered American and Canadian rechargeable lamp sets available. The most powerful (and versatile) lighting system is, however, British made. 'Starlites' provide up to 47W from a 12 volt gel-cell and, if you feel you can justify an outlay of about £150, then you will not be restricted to daylight for your cross-country cycling.

Manufacturers have been improving both the performance and efficiency of dynamos in recent years to get a higher, more reliable output. Some now have battery take-over systems to keep the lights on when the bicycle has stopped. The 'spoke' dynamo, recently introduced, is fitted to the hub and driven by an attachment to the spokes. This avoids the problem found with some tyre sidewall dynamos which can sometimes slip in wet and muddy conditions, though great strides have been made in overcoming this tendency.

A popular innovation in recent years has been the use of light-emitting diodes in cycle lights. These require little power and a couple of small batteries will last for hundreds of hours. This results in small, versatile units that can be fixed to helmets or armbands as well as the traditional light position on the bicycle itself. Unfortunately they are presently illegal as a primary light source, though they may well become accepted in the near future.

One way of making sure you are seen is to exploit motorists' lights by reflecting some of the light back. This is particularly useful on unlit country roads where the sudden flash of a reflector can be dramatic. Night-time visibility experiments conducted in 1984 by the Transport and Road Research Laboratory (TRRL) found that a good quality 'Sam Browne' reflective belt was readily seen at adequate distances by drivers even in conditions of urban glare. Moving reflectors grab the attention, so consider fitting pedal reflectors and wearing reflective trouser bands. The research by the TRRL also found that the most effective daytime conspicuity aid was a bright jacket. The percentage of drivers passing very close to a cyclist wearing such a jacket proved to be less than half that for a rider wearing a dark jacket. So if you're purchasing a jacket especially for cycling, make it a bright one.

Internal hub brakes are ideal for cross-country cycling. They are almost always more efficient than the standard rim-operating brakes, and are unaffected by the elements. They come fitted to some off-road bikes, but are generally too expensive for manufacturers to fit them at source. They have also had an image problem with the more macho mountain biker, for no explicable reason other than fashion.

Oddly, the law prohibits cycling on roads with lights more powerful than 3.6 watts. But if you like night riding off-road you can use British-made Starlites, which give out 47 watts, from a gel-cell rechargeable pack. In fact, many users consider the law to be an ass, and use these powerful lights on the roads. They cost around £150.

A recent innovation is the LED (Light-Emitting Diode) rear light. Despite their brightness, lightness, reliability and cheapness (hundreds of hours from two small batteries), these lights are illegal as a primary rear light for cyclists on British roads. Yet they are ideal for taking along for when you're caught by falling darkness on the way back from your ride in the hills.

25

CHAPTER FOUR

Planning a Ride

It is easy to plan an interesting and varied cross-country ride. All you need is a good map. Poring over maps to explore your own routes is as much an enjoyable part of the enterprise as the ride itself. However, if you wish to maximise the amount of off-road cycling on the trip, following a suggested route can help to reduce the complexities of navigation.

An ideal map is the Ordnance Survey Landranger 1:50,000 series on which all public rights of way are marked. (To explore an area in really close detail, use the OS Pathfinder map which has a scale of 1:25,000.) Some public libraries have complete sets of these maps available. Both map and key exhibit the clarity which has developed through 200 years of cartography since the first maps were made of south-east England for military purposes in 1790. They require no further explanation from us, but we have a few suggestions which may help if you are new to route planning.

Probably the most practical aspect is to learn to read contour lines so that you can judge how many steep ascents you will face during the ride, as well as how to avoid them if this revelation dismays you. They are drawn in brown, and lines packed close together indicate a steep hill. Where they are crossed by roads, hills are marked with single or double arrows, according to their steepness. The map of Rosedale shows several steep hills over the moors.

Look out for triangulation points, shown as little blue triangles with a dot, and ride close by them whenever possible. These are high spots from where early maps were planned and hence usually offer excellent views. Even a relatively short ride can leave you feeling on top of the world. When the heather is blooming we follow a route which takes in the thirty miles from York to Bransdale in the North Yorkshire moors. Then take a rough track along Rudland Rigg, descending past Toad Hole and Cowsike to the happily named Cockayne (imaginary land of idleness and luxury, according to the Oxford Dictionary). This off-road stretch might only last for some five miles in a round trip of about seventy, but the glorious panoramic view from the triangulation point looking over the heather-clad moor will easily stop you for an hour or two. Another rewarding treat is to ride across Begwns common, north-west of Hay-on-Wye in Wales. Although the triangulation point is

not particularly high at 414 metres, there are stunning views of the Black Mountains and other ranges.

Unless there is a specific prohibition you are generally allowed to cycle the long tracks across hill country or moor, which are marked as a pair of broken parallel lines but which don't carry the red bridleway markings. These have probably been used for many years by custom and, provided you take care, you won't cause any damage to these ancient tracks and will rarely meet a soul.

Allow plenty of time when exploring an unfamiliar off-road route; you can often meet with dead-ends where there is no observable way forward or find yourself faced with a field of crops or cattle. You will have to rework your route and may need to retrace part of your way. So leave yourself time to do this without getting into a lather.

We have been discussing cross-country routes using well-defined bridleways or tracks. If you attempt a more ambitious trip in a remote area, let someone know of your intended route, because if you have an accident you could be lost without trace for many hours.

The great potential of cycling as a leisure activity and tourist attraction is becoming recognised, and a host of local authorities are now producing cycle route maps suggesting rides that are all or partly off-road. Mass rides, often for charity, have shown that many more people will cycle if routes and facilities are provided for them. Avon County Council is now spending £300,000 a year on facilities for cyclists as a result of the popularity of the Bristol to Bath Cycle Route.

Routes are spreading from many locations. Thus the South Downs Way, opened twenty years ago as the first long-distance path with bridleway status, ran the eighty miles from Petersfield in West Sussex to Eastbourne in East Sussex. This route, which is suitable for cyclists, has now been extended to

Farleton Fell, near Kirkby Lonsdale: a section of the newly completed Cumbria Cycleway. Cumbria County Council have produced an excellent guide to the route. Many local authorities are now building good, largely off-road cycle routes, accompanied by good route guides.

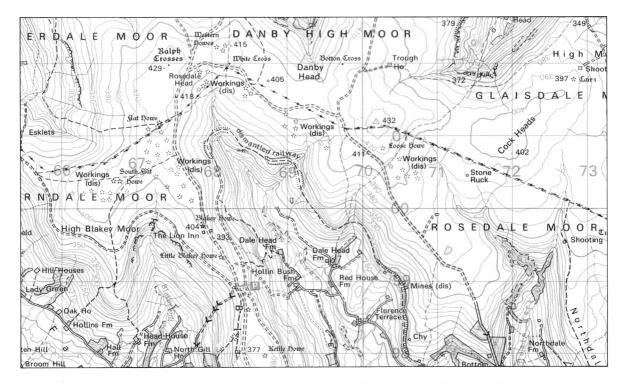

Monastic crosses, industrial archeology and dismantled railways. This map of part of the North York Moors shows it all.

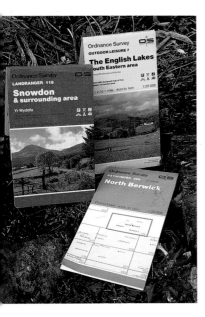

the west as far as Winchester. To the east, Wealden District Council has promoted the reconstruction of the partly derelict Cuckoo trail to provide a safe, attractive and traffic-free route for walkers and cyclists to Polegate, and northwards to Heathfield. This was built in partnership with Sustrans, the charity dedicated to the building of off-road paths for cyclists and walkers.

There are equally exciting developments at the other end of the country. In 1992 the Forestry Commission opened a new eleven-mile network of cycle routes through the Great Glenn from Inverness, along the length of Loch Ness to Fort Augustus. This gives cyclists an alternative to the busy A82 for part of the way from Fort William to Inverness, providing a safe and peaceful environment through Creag nan Eun and Porthclair Forests with spectacular mountain and loch views. A further twenty-four miles are planned. Cyclists are now welcome to cycle on forest roads in all the Forestry Commission woodlands of south-west Scotland (unless specifically advised otherwise). Over 200 miles of waymarked routes have been created in these forests, with a wide range of lengths and grades to suit all abilities. The cyclist will see not only trees but a whole mosaic of habitats, farmlands, burns, lochs, crags and open moorland, with some breathtaking views of the hills of Galloway and the Solway Coast.

The High Peak Trail in the Peak District runs for seventeen and a half miles from High Peak Junction near Cromford, to Downlow near Buxton. At Parsley Hay it is joined from the south by the Tissington Trail which runs for thirteen miles from Ashbourne. These former railway lines provide

walkers, cyclists and horseriders with fine scenic routes through the limestone countryside of the White Peak. The trails are owned by the Peak National Park authority and Derbyshire County Council, which purchased both routes after the closure of the railway in the late 1960s.

In Britain the weather is rarely bad enough to prevent anyone venturing out. Generally it is better to be out than in and, if you are wearing effective waterproofs, the showers don't seem as heavy as when you see them pattering against the window. Experiencing the weather at first hand can be most exhilarating but, however optimistic you may be, if you are going to spend most of the day in remote and exposed places following a new route you should attend more closely to the weather than if you are just pottering around country lanes. You may catch the detailed weather forecast on the radio before you set off, or phone the Weathercall number for a local report. Also, learn the skills of watching for changes in the weather while you are out riding:

Those high-flying cirrus clouds or mare's tails, for example, may look very beautiful against the blue sky but they can herald the arrival of wet weather with a warm front. Where a mass of warm air meets denser colder air, it rises and rides over the cold in a wedge shape, so the change first appears at the leading edge of the wedge at high altitude. Gradually cirrus will spread across the whole sky, veiling the sun, and altostratus cloud at a lower level will eventually obscure the sun with a grey blanket. If patches of wispy cloud

Part of the fun is being closer to the elements. Experienced cross-country cyclists read the clouds to see what's coming. *Photo courtesy Merril Footwear*

Opposite The three principal Ordnance survey maps used by cyclists. The purple Landranger is the most common, but the larger scale green Pathfinder is useful for shorter off-road rides where a richness of detail is appreciated. The large-scale yellow Outdoor Leisure maps cover only certain popular tourist areas.

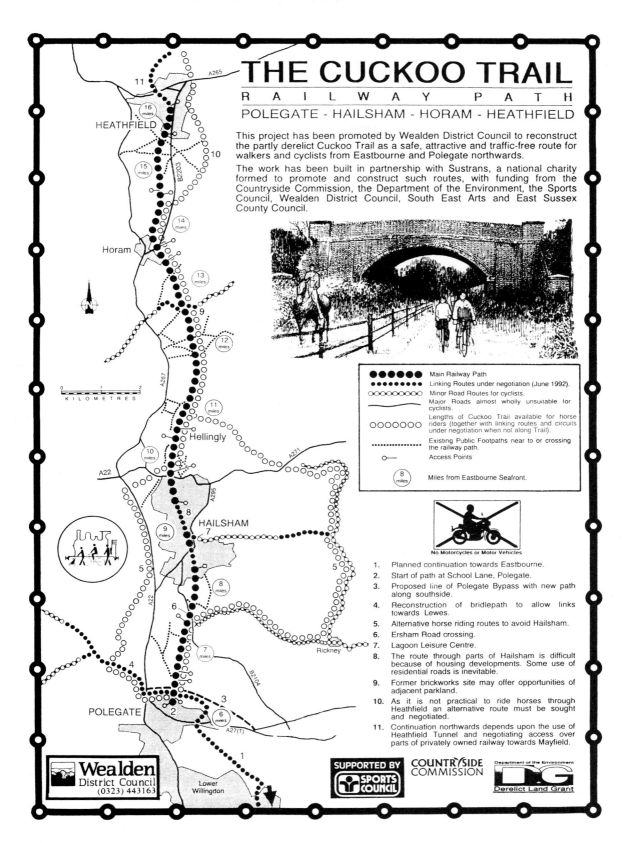

THE CUCKOO TRAIL
R A I L W A Y   P A T H
POLEGATE - HAILSHAM - HORAM - HEATHFIELD

This project has been promoted by Wealden District Council to reconstruct the partly derelict Cuckoo Trail as a safe, attractive and traffic-free route for walkers and cyclists from Eastbourne and Polegate northwards.

The work has been built in partnership with Sustrans, a national charity formed to promote and construct such routes, with funding from the Countryside Commission, the Department of the Environment, the Sports Council, Wealden District Council, South East Arts and East Sussex County Council.

●●●●●● Main Railway Path
•••••• Linking Routes under negotiation (June 1992).
∞∞∞∞∞∞ Minor Road Routes for cyclists.
———— Major Roads almost wholly unsuitable for cyclists.
○○○○○○○ Lengths of Cuckoo Trail available for horse riders (together with linking routes and circuits under negotiation when not along Trail).
•••••••• Existing Public Footpaths near to or crossing the railway path.
○— Access Points

(8 miles) Miles from Eastbourne Seafront.

No Motorcycles or Motor Vehicles

1. Planned continuation towards Eastbourne.
2. Start of path at School Lane, Polegate.
3. Proposed line of Polegate Bypass with new path along southside.
4. Reconstruction of bridlepath to allow links towards Lewes.
5. Alternative horse riding routes to avoid Hailsham.
6. Ersham Road crossing.
7. Lagoon Leisure Centre.
8. The route through parts of Hailsham is difficult because of housing developments. Some use of residential roads is inevitable.
9. Former brickworks site may offer opportunities of adjacent parkland.
10. As it is not practical to ride horses through Heathfield an alternative route must be sought and negotiated.
11. Continuation northwards depends upon the use of Heathfield Tunnel and negotiating access over parts of privately owned railway towards Mayfield.

Wealden District Council (0323) 443163

SUPPORTED BY SPORTS COUNCIL

COUNTRYSIDE COMMISSION

Department of the Environment
DG Derelict Land Grant

start blowing across below this layer, you can tell that there is a lot of water vapour up there which is shortly about to fall on you. As a guide for judging when to head for shelter, remember: the time it takes for the sun to be obscured after the high cirrus cloud first appears is about the same as the period between the disappearance of the sun and the start of rain. From the window of your hostelry you might observe the passing of the front by a band of light appearing on the horizon.

With the arrival of a cold front, the slope where the two masses of air meet is reversed with the cold air pushing under the warm. Thus clouds are piled up in the opposite order to the warm front. Its arrival may be obscured by low cloud, but against a clear sky you may see an approaching mass of majestic cumulo-nimbus clouds. Rain will clear as higher clouds appear, with cirrus marking the rear edge of the front. However this is not necessarily an all-clear as cumulus and cumulo-nimbus clouds often develop in the mass of cold air behind the front, leading to showers.

The above gives a general idea of what may happen when well-defined fronts arrive, though changes will be much less dramatic with the arrival of weaker fronts. The more you observe varying conditions, or consult weather guidebooks, the more accurate your predictions will become. Learning to read the weather, like learning to read a map, will improve your enjoyment of cross-country cycling.

The Moulton APB suitable for light off-road use, comes apart for storage in a car boot or on a train.

Getting yourself and your bike to good cross-country riding country can be difficult. British Rail has never been helpful. This Bike Bus, run by Harry Heneker of Edinburgh, is an alternative, and may set the pattern for the future.

It is unfortunate that cyclists who wish to enjoy the countryside without imposing their car on it can find it very arduous to get there in the first place. The rules about taking bikes on trains have become complicated and it is worth consulting an up-to-date leaflet on this subject. Some trains carry bikes free of charge, some carry none, while on others you have to book space in advance for a fee. The available space on many trains is the equivalent of a left luggage locker and will take only one bike. Families may have to travel on separate trains to take their bicycles on holiday with them. Perhaps one day we will have an ecologically-inspired, integrated transport policy which encourages the combination of rail and bike journeys.

There is more scope for travelling by train if you can transform your bike into luggage by dismantling it and carrying it in a transit bag. However the choice for the off-road rider has dwindled in recent years, leaving only the Moulton All-Purpose Bicycle, which is fine for moderate off-road jaunts. The Taiwanese company Dahon have designed a folding off-road bike which we believe will fit the bill. It is not yet imported as it has to be approved as meeting British Standards.

In some countries it is quite common for bikes to be carried on a bus or a coach. The Countryside Commission has recently supported a two-year experiment to get cyclists from Merseyside and Greater Manchester straight to the heart of attractive countryside in coaches adapted to take bicycles. This may well become a regular bus service. If the idea catches on there could be a whole series of bike-carrying services offering a relaxing and safe way of enjoying the countryside by bike. Just give us the chance!

CHAPTER FIVE

Personal Comfort

clothes and fuel

The fuel consumption of a cyclist is extremely low compared to any other form of transportation. In fact on a bicycle we are the most energy-efficient animal under the sun. This is because we propel ourselves using our strongest muscles in a smooth rotary motion. Moreover we do it sitting down, thus relieving some of the problems connected with our comparatively recently adopted posture – on an evolutionary timescale. When cycling slowly we use about a fifth of the energy that we need for walking, achieving the equivalent of 16,000 miles to the gallon.

However, this easy progress can lull us into a false sense of our capabilities with regard to our fuel needs. After spinning along happily for a good few

The most energy efficient form of transport. Yet the bicycle's human engine needs regular fuel and careful heat control.

Both rider and bicycle need regular lubrication for best performance. Your body can lose up to six pints of water during a day's ride.

miles, you may gradually begin to feel weak and wobbly if you have not stoked-up sufficiently. Suddenly your urgent priority is to locate a bar of fruit and nut from that most elusive of emporia, the village shop open on a Sunday afternoon. This is when you are showing red on your blood-sugar gauge, and you are a victim of what cyclists generally call 'the bonk' – running on empty – or hyperglycaemia. This crisis can be made worse by downing the contents of the sugar bowl at the village tea shop. A large amount of refined sugar, in any form, hitting the system suddenly, causes hyperglycaemia, which in turn induces a countering surge of insulin. This removes the sugar from the blood in order to store it, resulting in a renewed deficiency. It would be better to eat something like a large chunk of home-made fruit cake which will be digested gradually to provide a slow release of sugar into the blood. You can have the cream tea as well – after all you are on holiday.

To avoid getting into such a low state take a supply of munchables with you on your ride, particularly if you are riding cross-country, far away from any village. A bag of dried fruit and nuts is ideal as they won't squash or melt and the bag will fit easily into your luggage. This can be supplemented by a home-made flap-jack (made with a minimum or no refined sugar and

Sunshine and breeze.
Wearing layers of clothing
enables you to adapt to
changing weather conditions.

sweetened instead with concentrated fruit juice, or similar cereal and fruit
bar, and some fresh fruit as well. The sugar in fruit, whether fresh or dried
(fructose), is absorbed more slowly by the body than sucrose (refined sugar),
helping to maintain a steady energy level. A high carbohydrate meal before
you set off will build up energy stores (glycogens) for your trip and maintain
them throughout. Pasta, cereals, bread, potatoes and beans will all load
the glycogens with these energy-giving carbohydrates. Racing cyclists eat a
phenomenal amount of this type of food to keep their energy reserves topped
up. So start the day with a good breakfast and don't stint on the snacks.
Cycling is a wonderful excuse for a little self-indulgence.

In very hot weather the bonk can also be caused by an inadequate intake
of liquid. This is the comfort factor most commonly overlooked by the novice,
used to getting through the day on a few cups of tea or coffee. You can lose
up to six pints of water during a day's ride, so make sure you are equipped
with a full water bottle, and if you are a family group make sure the others
have one or two bottles as well. Replenish water bottles at every opportunity.
On very high ground you can often find an endless supply of delightfully
soft stream water but remember that the lower the altitude, the greater the
risk of contamination. In extreme circumstances salt loss can also be a prob-

lem, but generally the leisure cyclist will keep salt levels topped up with their snacks; and a packet of crisps at the pub stop won't go amiss.

We link clothing with fuel and energy because a good deal of the energy you have consumed will be lost as heat, and this heat-loss can be regulated by the clothing you choose. Cycling along at twelve miles an hour, you generate at least four times the heat you would if you were standing still. You won't necessarily feel particularly hot because you are cooled by the breeze. This is why exercise bikes are inferior to the real thing: they make you overheat and do not offer a cooling breeze.

In cold weather you need to dress in a way that best conserves the heat

Tourist shorts with pockets. Cycling gloves help with comfort, and protect the hands if you take a spill.

you are generating. This is done by wearing several thin layers of clothing between which the air is trapped; trapped air being the best insulator in this regard. Another practical reason for wearing several layers is that your temperature can vary quite considerably while you are cycling, depending on how much effort you are putting in: pedalling uphill will have you sweating, whereas you may become quite chilled as you zoom down the other side. A change in the weather and the need to use rainwear can alter your needs as well. A varied off-road ride may well involve several stops to add or remove clothing, excellent opportunities to enjoy the scenery.

One almost essential purchase for summer off-road riding is a good pair of shorts. Choose shorts designed for cycling which have reinforcements or padding at the seat and no raised seams to chafe. We recommend smart but traditional tourist shorts with roomy useful pockets, rather than skin-fit shorts. Many experienced cross-country cyclists carry a pair of thin, long trousers in their luggage, especially useful if you are cycling into unknown territory where routes may be overgrown with thorns, stinging nettles or the dreaded giant hogweed.

If you do have to wear waterproofs, especially in warm or mild weather, they tend to keep hot air trapped in, along with the moisture from your body. This is why breathable waterproof fabrics have become very popular in recent years. These fabrics let body moisture (which is in vapour form) out, while rain, in liquid form, cannot get through because of the fabric's surface tension. GoreTex is the most well-known brand and employs a microporous membrane. Other advanced proofings, many of which are just as good, employ the water-attractive or water-repellent properties of different molecular chains to provide the breathability. In contrast, Ventile is a more traditional material made of close, double-woven cotton, which is both weatherproof and 'breathes', working on the principle that when the cotton fibres become wet they expand, making the weave tighter still, while maintaining a microporous matrix through which moisture can escape.

If you are short of funds or have a favourite jacket that would be suitable if it were more waterproof, you can proof it easily at home with one of several proprietary treatments, such as Granger's Super-pel, or Nikwax TX10.

In cold weather you need to select the best kind of socks, hat and gloves. Because your feet are passive yet still wind-cooled, you need warmer socks than you would normally wear off the bike. A temporary solution is to wear two pairs of your normal socks, but ensure that your footwear is large enough to accommodate this extra layer. As with clothing, it is vital that the air is trapped around your feet and tight shoes will not only prevent this but will restrict your blood circulation as well, leading to even colder feet. Hats seem to have gone out of fashion for everyday use, but on a bike your head is wind-cooled, so get a good variety of hats to wear from a thin cotton one to a comfortably thick woolly one for winter. This will have a huge effect on your comfort, because the priority of your body-temperature control system is to maintain a constant temperature for the vital organs located in your

Above Skin shorts are popular amongst more competitive cyclists. Skins are designed to avoid chafing. Top class ones have chamois leather crotch pads; most have effective man-made crotch padding.

Below One of the many waterproof jackets now available to cyclists. They are almost all made of material which lets your sweat escape, in the form of water vapour, yet keeps the rain out.

A well-fitting cycle helmet stays firmly in position when you shake your head. No looseness should be felt.

Helmets come with pads of different sizes to adapt the interior to the oddities of your skull.

trunk and head. Your body will do this automatically, withdrawing heat from your extremities if necessary.

The adequacy of your everyday gloves will be sorely tested on a winter bike ride because they are stuck out in the wind and, like your feet, are passive. Numbness from cold can make you clumsy in handling the brake and gear levers. Seek out a pair of really warm gloves for winter conditions, yet which allow sufficient movement to work the gears. For other times of the year a pair of cycling mitts are a useful asset. They protect your hands if you have an accident and can make gripping the handlebars for longish periods more comfortable. Gloves and hat play a special role in body-temperature control because they are easily removed and replaced as your needs dictate. Your hat is especially valuable in this respect because you don't have to stop cycling to do this, and your head is the main conduit for heat-loss.

There is a great deal of fashionable cycle clothing available, much of which performs extremely well. Almost every major manufacturer or distributor has an off-road cycling shoe or boot in their range. A good bike shop will have a range of specialist footwear for you to try on.

Some cyclists argue for wearing 'normal' clothes on less demanding cross-country jaunts. This does have a cost benefit as well as reducing the 'wally factor'. If you do fancy traditional tweeds and moleskins, then the Hebden Cord catalogue is especially useful because they make specialist cyclist clothing (made to measure if you want), whereas other firms in the heartland of Yorkshire textiles supply a range of stylish, functional outdoor clothing. Hebden Cord are at Hebden Bridge, West Yorkshire, HX7 6EW.

There was a time when it seemed that practically every member of the Cyclists' Touring Club had a Ventile 'Greenspot' jacket, well faded after years of exposure to the elements. These are still obtainable direct from Bertram Dudley and Son, of Brooke Street, Cleckheaton, Yorkshire.

You can take the traditional look to the limit with deer stalker, plus-twos and brogues. However, for quality and design it is hard to beat the ranges of modern cycle clothing available in the more progressive cycle shops. Some even have changing rooms. Brogues make excellent cycling shoes, for the thick leather soles give excellent support across the pedals.

The soles of sporty-looking trainers not designed for cycling are likely to be too soft and your feet will suffer from every hard push against the unyielding pedal. For rough or muddy conditions you may want to choose cycling shoes with grip, such as those designed for mountain bikers, or you may find good walking shoes or boots fit your requirements. If your cross-country expeditions frequently take you into muddy terrain you may find that a good pair of wellies is the answer. They keep your feet dry and are useful in many other circumstances. Their major benefit is that they require virtually no looking after.

Helmets are a seemingly indispensable fashion item for young, athletic mountain bikers. For the competitive mountain biker they are a vital protec-

For a cooler day these Rohan striders bridge the gap between shorts and trousers. The light, windproof top, packs small for storage.

tion from the effects of high-speed falls, which are common. If you enjoy the frisson of risk and savour a turn of speed then buy a helmet. However we do not believe that helmet-wearing is necessary for more gentle cross-country riding, although you may habitually wear one for all your cycling activities. The helmet debate is a hot one. In itself cycling is not very dangerous. It is traffic conditions which create a threatening environment and make the cyclist feel vulnerable. Leisurely cycling, away from motor traffic, is a very safe pursuit. Many cyclists feel that helmet-wearing shifts emphasis and responsibility for safety away from the cause and on to the victim. Wearing helmets does not make traffic safer, nor improve the lives of the great non-motoring public.

A traditional Greenspot suit from Bertram Dudley. Double woven cotton fabric called Ventile expands when wet, making the material waterproof.

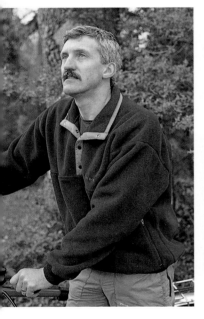

For Autumn and Spring riding: a warm fleece with an open neck for ventilation.

Buy a helmet from a shop that offers a good choice because sizing labels are often vague and unreliable. Ensure that it sits low on your forehead — you may have to sacrifice your hairstyle. Helmets often come with pads of different sizes which you can attach to the interior to accommodate the particular shape of your skull. Helmets can comply with a confusing array of safety standards for the many countries in which they are sold. Feel reassured by any of the following: British Standard (BS), American National Standard (ANSI), Snell Institute (a highly respected private American testing institute), Australian Standard (AS) and German (TUV).

Eat well, dress well and you'll ride well. Look after your body and out on your bike you'll feel on top of the world!

CHAPTER SIX

Equipment to Take

The way in which luggage is carried and distributed on the bike has a considerable effect on the way it handles and hence your enjoyment of the ride. Wobbly, insecure luggage will slow you down and become a constant irritation. Stable, well-made panniers at perhaps £80 for a large pair are likely to be your most expensive accessory. At prices like these, you might be tempted to pack everything into two large panniers and assorted improvised bags strapped to the top of the rear rack. Many of us started cycle touring in this way and thoroughly enjoyed our trips. However, with the rear end feeling as though it was transporting an unstable gas cooker, and the light front wheel bouncing off the road as we climbed steep hills, we had to admit there was room for improvement.

It is a generally accepted principle of on-road cycle touring that luggage should be evenly distributed between the front and rear of the bike, with panniers mounted low to keep the centre of gravity low. A contrary set of principles has evolved for off-road cycling. Low-mounted panniers are liable to catch on obstructions on narrow tracks, become muddy and wet, and prove an added burden if you have to lift or push the bike. So cross-country cyclists often use a small rucksack or a large 'bum bag' for day trips.

For day trips or less demanding rides, we prefer the medium-sized panniers which fit both front and rear carrier racks. In practice, this size of pannier is likely to be the most useful for your everyday cycling, rather than the large panniers which might be fine for a cycling holiday but are too voluminous for small amounts of luggage. If you intend to use a large pair for everyday use, ensure that they are adequately stiffened at the back and can be bound securely with straps so that they do not flap about when lightly loaded. Check that they are reinforced against wear at the back, where the bottom of the bag rubs over the lower attachment hook. Few bags are completely waterproof, so carry liners in case of a deluge. Some panniers convert into rucksacks, which is particularly useful if you intend to combine walking with cycling.

Good quality panniers are frequently made of woven nylon fabric such as cordura, but the traditional cotton duck material is still used. This is an extremely durable material that has proved its worth on countless

For day trips a simple pair of rear panniers carry the load.

Luggage for a long distance tour, with weight spread evenly front and back. The easily detachable bar bag is ideal for things which you need readily to hand, and for valuables which you do not wish to keep on the bike.

expeditions. It has a natural waterproofing quality for the threads swell when dampened, preventing water from soaking through. As there is a bewildering variety of bicycle luggage available and it can be an expensive outlay, we recommend that you shop around to familiarise yourself with the options. You could start by acquiring the brochures of three British manufacturers: Carradice, of St Mary's Street, Nelson, Lancashire BB9 7BA; Freedom Bike-packing, of Packers Cottage, Albion Street, Exeter, Devon EX4 1AZ; and Karrimor of Clayton-le-Moors, Accrington, Lancashire BB5 5JP. There are many other excellent pannier systems.

In addition to panniers for carrying the bulk of your luggage, there are different sorts of small bags which will disperse the load and be very useful for short trips. Many handlebar bags have an array of small interior and exterior pockets making them a good place to put your valuables as they are directly under your nose. This function is enhanced by the quick release fittings used by some manufacturers, which detach them from the bike in a second. These bar bags are not suitable for really rough riding because they would jiggle about a lot, distracting your attention and distressing the

contents. Edgar Newton finds his particularly useful for less demanding conditions when he can use them to carry items which he might need instantly, such as a camera or a map. Most bar bags have a transparent map pocket on top and some manufacturers supply additional padding to convert your handlebar bag into a camera bag.

An alternative to the bar bag is the trunk bag which has appeared in recent years to enable off-road riders to carry luggage on the top of pannier racks. These make good day-bags for general touring and often have the proliferation of useful pockets found in bar bags. They can carry more kit because their length is not as constrained as bar bags, which need to fit between drop handlebars. When buying a trunk bag make sure that the fittings can attach securely to your particular type of rack.

Racks have to be sturdy and securely attached to the bike. They will be more rigid if they fix at four points rather than having two bottom and one central fixing point. Aluminium is a popular material, being light and rust-free. Low-rider racks are favoured for the front of the bike as panniers mounted around the centre of the wheel have less effect on the steering.

If you are not carrying a bar bag with a map holder yet wish to follow a detailed and convoluted route, you can fix a map holder to the handlebars. If you have a simple sheet of route directions or a photocopied map, you can usually improvise by putting it in a plastic folder and clipping it with clothes pegs to the brake cables, or to a short elastic strap stretched between the brake hoods of a touring bike.

You need a fairly simple tool kit for a day ride: an adjustable spanner, tyre levers, a puncture repair kit, some Allen keys, a chain link extractor and a Swiss army knife. On a longer tour there is more time for something to work loose or go wrong, and carrying luggage submits your bike to greater stress. So take the tools for contingencies which you feel mechanically able to deal with: crank extractor, spoke key and freewheel-block remover, for

Below left A basic tool kit. Clockwise: adjustable wrench, rivet extractor for breaking the chain, puncture repair outfit, tyre levers, allen keys, screw drivers with spare cable tie, and (centre) a spoke key. *Below* Limpet panniers from Freedom Bikepacking. These innovative panniers convert into a rucksack when not on the bike.

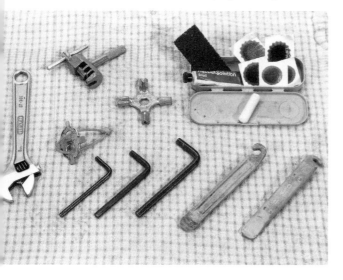

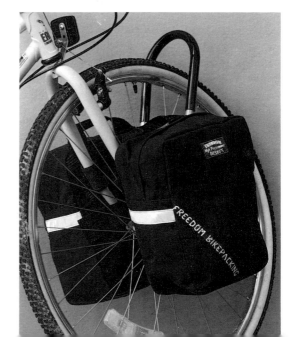

Touring the cycleways of Denmark. Although handlebar-mounted map holders are available, it's simpler to peg your map to the brake cables, as this cyclist has done.

example. Also carry some spares and extras for improvising solutions to unexpected breakdowns: a plastic film canister full of grease, some nylon cable ties, a few small nuts and bolts, some ball-bearings, strong string or nylon line, and a couple of elastic straps. When you are carrying a lot of luggage a few precautionary tools are not going to add much extra weight. As tools can rattle together, wrap them in a roll which you can easily make yourself out of an oddment of fabric – like denim. Fold it along one edge and sew this flap into pockets to hold each tool. Allow enough fabric at the other edge to fold down over the tools, and secure the roll with a stout rubber band. The tool roll will also provide a useful surface on which to lay small bits such as nuts, washers and ball-bearings when you are repairing the bike.

It almost goes without saying that the better the bike you buy and the more interest you take in cycle maintenance between rides, the less likely you are to have a problem miles from anywhere.

CHAPTER SEVEN

Riding Techniques

OK, so you're not the fastest thing on two wheels, but from the time you first learned to ride as a child, cycling has become second nature. The continual slight adjustments of your position to balance and change direction are demonstrations of the subtle skills that you have already mastered.

Cross-country cycling calls for a less subtle technique and your changes of position will need to be more radical to accommodate the more varied terrain. Over rapidly changing gradients mountain .bikers will sometimes

Lifting your body weight off the saddle adds to comfort and allows your bike to pivot freely over on even terrain.

Moving your body weight forward helps with hill climbing.

stand up in the saddle so that the bike can pivot more freely beneath them. Cycling up particularly steep hills can cause the front wheel to lift slightly. Try pedalling with your weight further forward by coming off the saddle and standing on the pedals, which will also help power you over the crest.

The most notable feature of the new generation of bikes is the vastly increased range of gears. Bikes now commonly have twenty-one or twenty-four gears, whereas touring bikes commonly had only ten before the birth of the ATB. The ease and rapidity with which you can change gear has been much improved by the introduction, a few years ago, of indexed gears, which change gear ratio with a distinct click. While you may be inclined to boast of the twenty-one or twenty-four gears on your bike, they will be of little use until you learn to deploy them effectively. No matter how well made, the derailleur gear remains essentially a simple device for pushing the chain from one sprocket to another. It does not incorporate a turbo charge or a power assist that will make you go faster. In practice you may find that you use only a couple of your many gears for cycling around town.

Most modern bicycles are equipped with three chain-rings (the larger toothed wheels driven by the pedals). Of these three the middle chainwheel is used most. One reason why manufacturers have increased the number of sprockets at the rear to eight is to widen the range that the middle chain-ring can offer, so that most cyclists can pootle around all day on this ring alone. It is most efficient if you can keep up the same pedalling rate (cadence) even while going slowly, to maintain a smooth rhythm which suits you and does not stop when your foot reaches the point of minimum leverage (at the top and bottom of the stroke). There is no virtue in propelling yourself with mighty thrusts of the pedals in a high gear, straining your joints and muscles. Practise pedalling at a smooth, rapid rate in the course of your everyday cycling. The ideal cadence is about 90 revolutions per minute. You can easily measure 15 revolutions per ten seconds with your watch while practising this. After practice, you will probably settle down to a habitual rate that is somewhat slower, though you may well find you have increased your pace without greater effort. Toe-clips help you to maintain a smooth rate of pedalling by keeping your foot correctly positioned. If you choose to use them, slipping in and out of them will soon become second nature to you.

When riding off-road it helps to change down a couple of gears in advance of any obstacle which you think may slow you down. A steep incline or deep muddy patch will require this technique, and especially riding through deep water.

Many cyclists have an instinctive caution that makes them brake when confronted by a hazard. However you should try to plough through without braking if possible. Search out the line ahead, looking for the one that gives the most traction. You are likely to have pretty powerful brakes on your cross-country bike which may lock the wheels in a skid on a slippery surface. Learn the gentle touch, using the front brake less than the rear, because

Three chainrings. If your ride is not too demanding you can stick to the middle chainring at the front, and use the wide range of gears available at the back. Seven sprocket rear blocks are now common, and eight sprocket blocks are coming in.

Above left Showing off. Moving your body weight backwards gives more control on descents. *Above* Look ahead, to search out a line which gives best traction.

plainly if the front wheel stops completely on mud you will lose steerage, and on less slippery surfaces you risk airborne progress!

If you are venturing off-road for the first time, it will be a little like first learning to cycle, when you overreacted and wobbled or braked because you felt the machine would run away from you. Relax and you will learn to have fun in rough conditions. Adjustment of weight and alignment will soon become second nature.

CHAPTER EIGHT

Routes and Your Rights

Rights of way provide essential access, allowing us to enjoy parts of the countryside otherwise denied us in this small, densely populated land, obsessed since feudal times with the rights of landowners. Many of these tracks were the highways of medieval Britain, connecting villages and hamlets, paths to work or to worship, or long-distance trading routes used by packhorses or drovers taking animals to the cities. Many have fallen into disuse and become completely overgrown, effectively disguised to discourage access. Even experienced cyclists navigating with Ordnance Survey maps are frequently at a loss to know where to proceed. So it's important to know your rights.

Other country-lovers have rights as well as cyclists, and it is vital that cyclists behave sensitively when encountering walkers, horseriders, and anxious landowners.

All public rights of way are highways in law. Anyone can use them at any time, just as you would any other highway. This is indeed a right not a privilege granted by the landowner, so you should not be intimidated and denied access. It is, however, essentially a right of passage across land, and it does not allow you to strike off from the track or engage in activities unconnected with travel that may cause disturbance to people or animals. The kind of passage you are allowed depends on the status of the highway:

A public right of way is exactly that: a right, not a privilege granted by a landowner.

* A footpath is a highway over which the public has a right of way on foot only.
* A bridleway is a highway over which the public has a right of way on foot, on horseback or on a pedal cycle.
* A Byway Open to All Traffic (BOAT) is a highway over which the public is entitled to travel on foot, horseback or pedal cycle and by wheeled vehicles of all kinds (including horsedrawn), but is used by the public mainly for walking or for riding.

Cyclists on bridleways must give way to horseriders and walkers. You have clear rights of way, but you may be unsure of where these apply. Fortunately you have a number of allies in exercising your rights. The Countryside Commission (see p.96) is committed to improving the access to and enjoy

If you are not sure about the legality of access restrictions, you can consult the definitive rights of way map held by your local council.

ment of rights of way, and many local authorities are keen to develop them as leisure facilities in their area. You may frequently follow a sign which indicates a bridleway at the point where it leaves the metalled road, and then rapidly lose your way. To prevent this a system of waymarking is being developed to provide simple signs along such routes. The recommended system in England and Wales uses small arrows to show the direction of the path. A different colour is used for each category of right of way:

* Footpaths are waymarked with yellow arrows.
* Bridleways are waymarked with blue arrows.
* Byways Open to All Traffic (and other routes that may legally be used by wheeled vehicles) are waymarked with red arrows.

Ordnance Survey Pathfinder and Landranger maps show all public rights of way. The Countryside Commission produces a leaflet entitled *Waymarking Public Rights of Way*, which gives guidance on the design and location of signs for groups who might want to improve routes.

Cyclists are not restricted to riding on public rights of way, but are allowed to use the following by local or established custom or by special consent:

* Many areas of open country, like mountain, moorland, fell and coastal areas, especially those of the National Trust, and also commons (unless specifically disallowed by local by-laws).
* Some woods and forests, especially those owned by the Forestry Commission where special cycling routes have been created.
* Some towpaths on canals and rivers for which you will need to buy an annual permit.
* Some private tracks where special access agreements exist.

However, on most of your off-road excursions you will be using bridleways, and if you find one to be obstructed or badly marked you can take action to remedy the situation. Your first step should be to contact the local authority responsible for protecting and maintaining rights of way. Its duties include maintaining the surface, signposting and preventing obstruction. In this case the highway authority will be the county, metropolitan district or London borough council for the area. In addition district and parish councils have important discretionary powers, allowing them to work with those highway authorities to manage, protect and maintain rights of way.

The highway authority is also charged with the preparation of a 'definitive'

Cyclists share bridlepaths with pedestrians. In recent years aggressive riding by some mountain bikers has caused resentment amongst ramblers.

51

Having the right of passage across a piece of land does not give you the right to leave the path and strike off where you will. Nor are you allowed to cause disturbance to people or animals.

Opposite By local custom, cyclists are allowed to use many areas of open country, especially if it's common land.

map showing all the public rights of way in the area. This map must be available to look at, free of charge, at reasonable hours. District councils usually havè one available that covers the district. These maps are constantly modified to show recent changes such as building developments. They are thus likely to be more up to date than the available Ordnance Survey maps. (It was through checking the local definitive map that we discovered a quiet and traffic-free back route: a public bridleway which runs beside a golf course. It's a very convenient route and we whizz along it regularly, happy to weather the frosty stares of the petulant putters.)

Keep abreast of large-scale new developments in your area, for if you lobby planning authorities in time, they could ask developers to maintain or introduce access for cyclists as a condition for planning permission.

If you find you have problems with local rights of way, especially those within urban areas, write to the local highway authority about these short-comings or contact a local councillor direct. In an age of citizens' charters where local authorities are supposed to be responsible to their consumers, there are many local authority officers who would welcome the opportunity

The Forestry Commission are opening up entire networks of forest trails to public access. This one is near Peebles, in the Scottish Borders.

to consult with an authentic citizen. Some authorities have specialists, such as cycling officers, who would obviously be your first point of contact.

When they first appeared in 1981 many regarded mountain bikes as a threat. Nowadays, most of the large authorities responsible for managing land in the country see cross-country cycling as a legitimate leisure pursuit. The British Mountain Bike Federation has helped to encourage this positive approach. It aims to create the right environment for everyone to be able to cycle off-road and has created a network of volunteer Access Officers, one for each county and one for each National Park. These officers liaise with land managers, local authorities and other user groups. Their efforts have borne fruit: in the Snowdonia National Park, for example, a voluntary access agreement has been reached. The Forestry Commission has been particularly positive and is constantly opening up new areas. For example, the Forest of Dean now successfully accommodates vast numbers of mountain bikers. Indeed the BMBF is aware of 700 such cross-country routes in England and Wales, and to maintain this constructive approach to mountain biking it has drawn up the following code. While some of it is not applicable to the more leisurely rider, it is nevertheless a useful and well-worded code of conduct, designed to promote enjoyment and a sense of responsibility:

THE OFF-ROAD CYCLING CODE

1 Stay on the trail
Only ride bridleways and byways
Avoid footpaths
Plan your route in advance
Use the Pathfinder/Landranger
maps

2 Give way to horses and walkers
Make sure they hear your
approach
Ride carefully when you pass

3 Bunching is harassing
Ride in twos and threes

4 Be kind to birds, animals and
plants
Keep your dog under control

5 Prevent erosion
Skids show poor skills

6 Close gates behind you
Don't climb walls or force hedges

7 Stay mobile
Wear a helmet
Take a first-aid kit
Carry enough food and drink
Pack waterproofs and warm
clothes

8 Take pride in your bike
Check it before you leave home
Take essential spares and tools

9 Be tidy
Take your litter home
Guard against fire

10 Keep smiling, even when it hurts.

It is sometimes hard to tell whether or not cycling is permitted on a path. This cliff-top path above the Tweed in Coldstream is wide, little used, and avoids the busy high street. Local cyclists use it carefully, and there have been no complaints.

CHAPTER NINE

Bicycle Adjustment and Overhaul

A well-used bike needs fairly frequent tuning and maintenance if it is to perform at its best. However the transparency of bicycle technology makes this relatively easy to do yourself. Once this becomes routine you will recognise problems before they arise and so take remedial action which will keep your bike running smoothly at all times. You will find yourself riding along, in tune with this wonderful machine with nary a clatter or a clunk to distract you.

The brakes are subject to a great deal of crude force, so check the cables for signs of wear or fraying at both ends and where the inner wire passes through guides. It is a sensible and cheap precaution to replace the brake cables from time to time even if there is no apparent wear, greasing them before threading them through the outers. Check the brake blocks for wear and replace them long before the rim is exposed to the metal of the brake shoe. Make sure that the blocks engage squarely with the rim and check, too, that there is no chance that they can rub the tyre, because it is devastatingly easy to ruin an expensive new tyre in this way. You should adjust the brake blocks so that they are close to the rim, without rubbing.

Cables are adjusted so that, when the brakes are applied they engage before the levers have travelled so far that they are near to the handlebars. This adjustment is made with a barrel adjuster at the end of the cable casing, either on the brake lever or on the brake calliper, which you should screw in to make the cable looser or unscrew to make the brake cable more taut.

If your brakes shriek like a banshee when you pull them on, the brake blocks have to be toed-out slightly so that the trailing end hits the rim first. On cantilever brakes you will find a system of curved washers which allows this adjustment, whereas with side-pull brakes you can *carefully* bend the callipers in the jaws of an adjustable spanner. Alternatively, fit a different make of brake block.

The modern rear derailleur mechanism is mechanically a relatively simple device which pushes the chain from one sprocket to another. It incorporates adjustable stops to prevent it from throwing the chain over either side of the sprocket cluster. These stops are simply two small projecting screws which

Doing your own maintenance gives you a deeper appreciation of the wonder that is your bicycle.

are marked H and L, denoting which end of the range the screw affects: H = High end; L = Low end. Index gears, which move the chain from one sprocket to another with a click of the gear lever, require very careful adjustment which is best done by following the manufacturer's instructions.

The end of the cable is clamped to the mechanism with a bolt and the fine tuning is done with the barrel adjuster situated where the cable enters the mechanism. Before adjusting this, check that there is no slack in the cable when the chain is on the smallest cog at the back. Shift the chain on to the next sprocket: if it will not go or if it overshifts, tension or loosen the cable by slightly turning the barrel adjuster. Then move the chain back and

forth across the middle sprockets, making minor adjustments on the barrel adjuster until the chain runs smoothly on these. This is best done with the chain set on the middle ring of a triple, or on either of a double. This adjustment can sometimes require the sensitivity of a safe-cracker.

The front gear mechanism can similarly be limited in its sideways travel with the throw-adjuster screws and adjusted with the barrel adjuster on the shifter.

Your chain obviously has a fairly punishing time, being pushed from sprocket to sprocket, especially if you are riding in conditions which will throw a lot of dirt or mud in the works. It will stretch over time and in turn can start wearing down the chainwheels and sprockets. Check for wear by pulling a link away from the teeth at the front of the chain-ring. If it pulls away more than 5mm, or enough to expose a whole tooth on the chain-ring, discard it. You can remove and replace a chain with a link extractor tool. Be careful not to push a link right out, but leave it retained in one side of the chain. When replacing a chain, check that the link you have fitted is not stiff. You can loosen it with the extractor tool, or by flexing the chain laterally. The wider chains which go with hub chains are broken and joined together again by means of a 'split link'. This comes apart once you have prised off a surclip with a screwdriver. Replace the surclip with its open end to the rear.

The chain can be removed to be cleaned, there are now a number of solvents that can be used to clean chain, chainwheels and gear block. When everything is clean and dry, spray lubrication on the chain and block as you run the chain backwards.

We now turn to giving your bike a more systematic overhaul, by taking internal fittings apart. The frequency with which you need to work on your bike will depend on how often and how hard you use it. Mountain bike racers might clean and adjust their bikes after every ride. A bike that is used for leisure rides and holidays will need a basic overhaul only once a year, with gear and brake adjustment and lubrication as the need arises.

Below A strap from a toe clip is an improvised way of holding brake blocks close to the rim while you make adjustments. You can also buy a simple tool called a 'third hand'. *Below right* Adjusting the stops on derailleur gears, preventing the chain from being thrown off either side of the sprocket cluster.

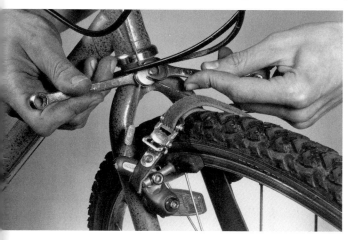

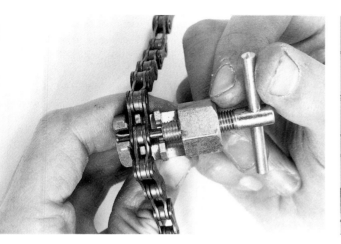

You will enjoy maintenance more if you can work in comfortable conditions. Raise the bike up to a height where you can work on it without stooping, either putting it on a workbench protected against dirt and grease, or perhaps hanging it from the garage rafters. If you have a Black and Decker Workmate, you can fit it with a Kestrel Workmate bicycle stand. If space indoors is limited, you can use a portable workstand outside, planning your overhauls for the warmer weather.

You could be saving yourself service charges in the region of £15 per hour by doing your own maintenance, so invest some of this saving into good quality tools for the job. Buy a well-made adjustable spanner (without excessive play in the jaws) and gradually acquire separate spanners for the common nut sizes on your bike, especially the fiddly little nuts on brakes – it is all too easy to round these off with an ill-fitting spanner. A Y-shaped three-headed socket spanner is excellent here, as it provides firm support for nuts that are difficult to get at. Cable cutters are useful for making clean breaks in gear and brake cables, but if necessary you can get away with using the cutting edges of a good pair of pliers. Press through the wires with one brute squeeze; do not waggle them or the end of the cable will fray.

Find an array of plastic pots and bowls to keep small parts in, and perhaps a larger tray on which everything can be cleared away should maintenance spread over several days. Keep those old toothbrushes and use a soft dustpan brush for cleaning the chain, sprockets and gears.

As your first step in the overhaul, take your front wheel apart. It involves taking apart the ball-bearing assembly, and these are also found in the rear wheel, bottom bracket, pedals and headset. This elemental simplicity is complicated on some more expensive machines where sealed cartridge bearings are used in some casings, for these are not meant to be serviced or removed by the average home mechanic.

On a standard ball-bearing set up, the balls run around a cup inside the end of the hub, and are held in place by a threaded cone on the axle. This

Above left To remove the kind of chain used with derailleur gears you need to break it by means of a link extractor. Do not push the rivet right out, or you'll have trouble getting it back again. *Above* Spray lubrication on the chain and block, running the chain backwards as you do so.

is fixed in place with a lock nut. To loosen the front hub, you hold the cone with a cone spanner, which is thin enough to fit under the lock nut, and then undo the lock nut with another spanner. Remove both cone and lock nut and any intervening washers and take the axle out, holding the wheel above a pot to catch any bearings that fall out. Dirt seals over the bearings can be levered out of the hub with a screwdriver. Count the bearings as they come out, as they are easily lost when you are cleaning them. Clean the ball-bearings, cone and the bearing cups (in the hub) and check for any signs of irregular wear or pitting, which will require replacement parts.

After the parts are clean and dry, spread grease around the bearing cups, into which you bed the bearings and then spread more grease over them. Press the dust seals back into the axles. Carefully slide the axle into the hub and replace the cones, washers and lock nut. Screw the cone down against the ball-bearings, until the wheel can revolve freely, but with slight looseness. Then lock the cones in place with the lock nuts, using your cone spanner and ordinary spanner. This is fine tuning, so you might need to loosen and adjust again before you are satisfied.

You can now apply the same procedure to the rest of the bike. Adjustable pedals have a dust cap which can be removed to reveal the same cone and lock nut set up. The cone is freed by turning the axle, while a screwdriver holds the cone fixed, either by being wedged against the side, or located in a slot on top of the cone. You need to take the pedals off in order to work on them. The left hand pedal screws into a left-hand thread in the crank, but, as an *aide-mémoire*, 'the right hand pedal screws in the right way'. The small ball-bearings in pedals are a fiddle to work with but you can marshal them by picking them up with the tip of a magnetic-tipped screwdriver (many pozidrive screwdrivers are magnetic) or an ordinary screwdriver dipped in grease.

The rear wheel has a similar set up to the front, but you might need to remove the freewheel with the appropriate tool, otherwise the bearings on the block side are difficult to get at; although not impossible, because you

Below Front wheel locknut being removed, while a cone spanner holds the cone. *Below right* The cone comes out. The bearings are still hidden by the dirt seal at the end of the hub. This can be levered out with a screw driver.

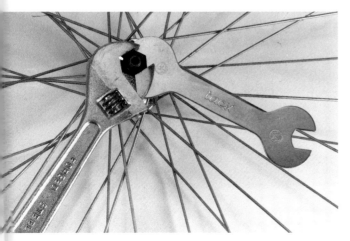

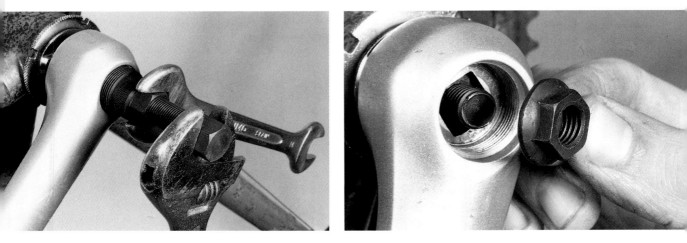

can reach through to clean the cups using a toothbrush or a rag wrapped around a screwdriver.

Look at the left-hand side of the bottom bracket and you will see a lock ring around the edge of the removable cup – the normal configuration is reversed, with the cups rather than the cones being removable. You need a C spanner to remove the lock ring, or if you are a '*rude mechanical*', the delicate application of a punch or stone chisel. Then lean the frame on its side to remove the cup, while pulling the axle up to keep the bearings in place against the cup as they love to disappear down the depths of the frame tubes. Clean, regrease and replace the components, remembering that the longer end of the axle goes in first through the fixed cup to carry the chainwheels. Sealed bearing units are becoming common and any servicing of these needs to be done by a bike shop. You need to put a crank back on to test whether there is any play in the bottom bracket by levering against it.

Another set of ball-bearings is found in the headset. Take great care how you disassemble this or a whole crowd of small bearings might stage the great escape.

The cranks are taken off the bottom bracket axle by means of a crank-remover. To operate this, you remove the dust cap in the end of the crank. Remove the nut and thrust the washer holding the crank on to the end of the axle with a socket spanner which is sometimes found at one end of the crank tool. You then screw the collar of the crank tool right into the recess of the crank. Check that it is in as far as it will go, because it is easy to strip the soft aluminium threads inside a crank. Then screw in the bolt of the crank tool so that it presses against the axle, forcing the crank off.

The modern bicycle is a miracle of engineering. By learning to maintain and repair your bicycle you will better appreciate its subtleties and its strengths, and enjoy the added satisfaction of self-sufficiency.

Above left Removing an alloy crank. Screw the crank tool right into the recess before screwing the bolt to push the crank off the axle. *Above* The threads inside alloy cranks are easily stripped if you don't screw the crank tool right in.

Below There is a ball race either side of the bottom bracket axle.

CHAPTER TEN

Off-Road Cycle Paths

towards a network

Some of the most exciting developments in off-road cycling in this country have been the work of Sustrans, a charity devoted to the construction of cycle paths and the conversion of redundant railway paths for pedestrian and cycle use.

This began in 1979 when John Grimshaw designed the first path for a group of cycle enthusiasts and campaigners in Bristol. The first five miles of the Bristol and Bath railway path were built in three months by enthusiastic volunteers with funds they had raised themselves. The simple construction methods have been applied elsewhere, with the government-funded job creation programmes providing much of the labour, until 1989 when such programmes ceased. Sustrans has now constructed over 250 miles of cycle paths and is promoting a further 1000 miles of potential cycle routes. Completed tracks include Selby to York, Bath to Bristol, Consett to Sunderland, and Glasgow to Loch Lomond. The innovative Bristol to Bath track now accommodates over a million journeys a year.

The long-distance routes which Sustrans promotes are not necessarily entirely off-road. Some involve on-road cycle facilities such as cycle lanes. These are vital links, allowing safe access for townsfolk to the countryside. Sustrans lays particular importance on these links, which offer locals as well as tourists the benefit of safe riding. The planned Trans-Pennine trail, from Hull to Liverpool and Southport, passes through the northern urban corridor with thirteen million people living within reach of this transit facility. It was developed as a result of a report commissioned by Barnsley District Council to look at disused rail routes. Sustrans saw that the route could be extended to York. A further extension to Liverpool to the west and then to Humberside and Hull to the east, means that a total of thirty-six local authorities, organised into area groups, are now involved.

Another example of an excellent route giving city cyclists easy and safe access to the countryside is the Plym Valley Cycleway which runs from Laira Bridge, Plymouth, along the attractive wooded valley of the river Plym to Goodameavy, at the edge of the Dartmoor National Park.

All Sustrans paths are constructed to a very high standard with either an asphalt or a limestone chip and dust surface. They are generally two to three

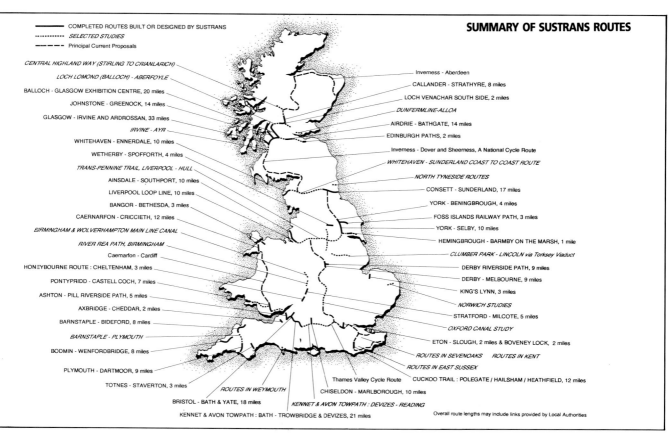

metres wide, cambered, and raised if flooding is likely to be a problem. All access points are designed to enable wheelchair and pushchair users to join the path, while keeping motor-cyclists out. The paths are usually set in a wonderful natural landscape, which can often be a wildlife corridor. Where the original railway line was on an embankment with houses on one or both sides, the path is sunk into the embankment and 'privacy banks' are formed from the resultant spoil.

Every encouragement is given to the cyclist to enjoy the ride. Sustrans intends to install an individual work of sculpture to mark each mile. One of the most dramatic is the sculpture marking seventeen miles on the Glasgow to Loch Lomond trail, which features seventeen Roman soldiers marching down on the line, bearing the number 17 as their standard. Another is the Worm, a quarter of a mile long earthwork designed by Andy Goldsworthy, on the Consett and Sunderland path. On the Bristol and Bath sculpture trail some of the sculptures were made by school groups, by people with disabilities, and by members of drop-in centres and women's groups.

Tracks such as these offer safe and pleasant mobility which has elsewhere vanished under the dominance of motor traffic. Lost is the freedom enjoyed by children born in the 1940s and 1950s to roam on foot or by bicycle as an important step to independent adulthood. Children's freedom is restricted not only by the direct physical danger that motor vehicles pose, but also by

Many Sustrans paths have acted as a catalyst to further safe routes in local areas. These are not shown on this map.

the increased mobility of disturbed adults. Partly as a result of this, children's fitness is at an all-time low. The national popularity of sedentary indoor entertainment is leading to a generation of children whose bodies are becoming atrophied. It is disappointing to note that more than 90 per cent of junior schoolchildren own bikes yet few use them as a form of transport. But visit a local Sustrans track on a fine day soon after Christmas and you will see many families with very young children proudly wobbling along on their favourite present.

One of Sustrans' current plans is to connect a number of trails and other routes to create a 1000-mile cycle route from Inverness to Dover which will encourage a whole range of cycling activities. They estimate that the route will carry upwards of twenty million journeys per year (based on usage figures for routes already constructed). They envisage commuter travel, family leisure cycling, sports cycling, mass rally events, long-distance adventure travel, training in responsible cycling, and travel to school. On the south coast end of the route, Sustrans is devising some very attractive routes, following the sea front where possible, by making use of promenades through urban areas and minor roads elsewhere. At Bexhill, for example, the local authority has already built a special section of asphalt cycle path on the shingle and it is planned to extend it as far as Hastings. The section between Rye and Hythe may use the towpath of the Royal Military Canal for part of the way. To open up a quiet route in East Kent for local residents as well as foreign visitors, Dover District Council is considering continuing the path along a railway path which was used during the Second World War to move artillery up to the cliffs.

It is hoped that this national route will form part of the growing European network of national long-distance cycle routes, connecting British cyclists via sea crossings to the two existing Fietsrouten (cycle routes) which run

A section in Cardiff of the Three Castles Routes. Sustrans routes are a lifeline into the surrounding countryside.

The Three Castles Route, built by Sustrans in South Glamorgan.

the entire length of the Dutch coast. This in turn connects with Radweg 1 which leads on to the many German cycle routes. Holland and Denmark, and to some extent Germany, have developed an extensive network of routes on both minor roads and special cycle paths.

Sustrans is a small but highly efficient charity doing an excellent job. But Britain as a whole is lagging behind other European countries in the official provision of cycle facilities. Austria, for example, a country often regarded as best suited to alpine pursuits, boasts a 300km cycle track along the Danube Valley. In many ways Austria is rapidly becoming one of the most cycle-friendly countries in Europe. Bicycles may be rented from 167 railway stations throughout the country, and returned to any other station (similar facilities are available in Switzerland). The Danube track takes cyclists

Off-road cycling in the Netherlands. A cycling holiday in the Netherlands or Denmark is ideal for anyone new to cycling. Only a miracle of political will could ever give British cyclists facilities such as these.

through Vienna which is alive with bicycles. The city has parking places for 5000 bicycles, hire facilities at three rail stations and at three car parks, and there is also a Bicycle Office to advise cycling visitors. Many of the tree-lined boulevards around the city have cycle tracks.

Some twenty-five kilometres from Vienna you can ride through vineyards on a network of cycle routes, each marked by little green signs beside the track, and sometimes by directions painted on the track itself. These days you can pedal further, into Hungary, for example, since border crossings are now thrown open to cyclists from spring to autumn during daylight.

Long-distance routes in Britain will benefit local people as well as attract visitors to the area who are far more likely to linger there than if they had to come and go by car.

What does all this mean to the beginner cyclist? Surfaced off-road cycle tracks are an ideal way to travel safely and enjoyably off-road. In Britain there are as yet very few, although Sustrans look like being a major force in this area before the end of the decade. Such paths are ideal for newcomers to cycling. But if there are no Sustrans paths near you then you might consider trying out the many excellent cycle path networks abroad. We list appropriate cycle holiday companies in Chapter 17. At the same time it's well worth supporting Sustrans in their work. As a charity they are always in need of voluntary 'path wardens', and you can probably help them build new paths too. Contact details in Chapter 17.

CHAPTER ELEVEN

Breakages and Bruises

field repairs and first aid

When you bounce along rough tracks you subject your bike to considerable stresses. These will be exacerbated if you choose to load it with heavy panniers rather than a daypack. Unusual problems occur, usually when you least expect them, so it pays to have a few tricks up your sleeve for dealing with them.

When something goes wrong your first reaction may be to curse in exasperation, but allow yourself time to think and consider your resources – you may be able to bodge together a solution which will, at least, allow you to ride home slowly. Here are some techniques which may help.

The rear gear mechanism, mounted as it is in an exposed position near to the ground, can be knocked and bent out of action. If this happens you can employ a single gear by removing the damaged mechanism and running the chain round a sprocket in the middle of the cluster, giving you a middling gear. You can choose a larger sprocket if you need an easier get-you-home gear, or a smaller one if you can cope with a harder ride. You'll need to remove some links from the chain so that it is not too slack. It is therefore important to carry a chain tool and know how to use it.

If one of your gear cables breaks you can run the chain on to one of the middle sprockets at the back if it is the rear cable, or the middle chain-ring at the front if it is the front cable which is broken. Do this by setting the throw-adjusting screws on either gear-changing mechanism, to limit the movement of the mechanism. If it is the rear gear that is affected you can continue changing gear with the front mechanism, because the jockey cage will maintain chain tension. And this principle applies equally if the front mechanism is the one which needs to be fixed in one position.

If you are unfortunate enough to buckle a wheel so badly that it will not turn within the frame or forks, some crude measures may just get you home. Lay the wheel on the ground or against a solid object and force it back to shape. This is likely to leave loose as well as overtaut spokes, so with a spoke key try to even the spoke tensions up. You will probably have to adjust the brakes so that the blocks clear the wobbles when the wheel goes round.

If a spoke breaks, you can live with it until you get home, but if several

Field repairs can make the difference between riding home and walking home.

go you need to replace them if possible. This is difficult if some are on the freewheel side of the rear wheel. It will necessitate removing the sprockets to gain access to the spoke holes. You can do this with some freewheels (sprocket clusters) by fixing the larger sprockets to the spokes with a length of wire or cloth and with the chain set on to the smallest sprocket, stamping on the pedal in a reverse direction. It is wisest to carry a cassette cracker suitable for your make of freewheel.

Always carry a spare inner tube with you, but if you also run out of patches after suffering multiple punctures, you can knot the tube to seal off the punctured section. If you are a patient soul you could make a sleeve joint by slicing clean through the inner tube and gluing one end inside the other, using the sandpaper from your repair kit to roughen the adjoining

faces. If a slow and soft ride might be preferable to walking, you can pack the tyre with grass or straw.

The side-walls of modern tyres are usually pretty thin and can easily suffer a split. In this case you need to devise some method of restraining the inner tube with card or cloth, or if you have a large puncture patch glue that over the inside of the split, after cleaning the area very thoroughly indeed.

Small bolts can sometimes go missing, particularly at the lower attachment points for carrier racks. You can substitute a plastic cable tie, or a piece of wire which can be twisted taut with pliers, or use a metal tyre lever (or the shank of a screwdriver) if you form the wire into a suitable loop. If the rack itself breaks, you can lash it together, perhaps using a spanner or Allen key as a splint. Broken frame tubes and handlebars can also be held by a splint after first ramming a length of wood into the broken ends.

If you ride carefully, anticipating the line to take between and over obstacles, you are unlikely to come to serious grief. However you are supposed to be having fun, which tends to encourage exuberance, and occasional careless-

Above left If your rear derailleur is damaged you remove it entirely and run the chain on the middle sprocket of the cluster. *Above* If a split in your inner tube is too large to patch, you can often make do by tying a knot in the tube.

Below left Serious stuff – a broken handlebar reinforced by having a piece of wood rammed into it, and braced with a spanner. *Below* Nuts and bolts which have worked loose can be replaced with plastic ties or pieces of bent metal.

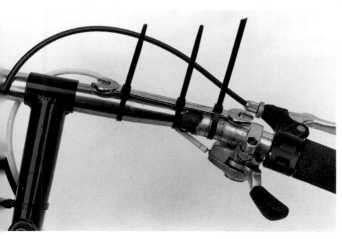 

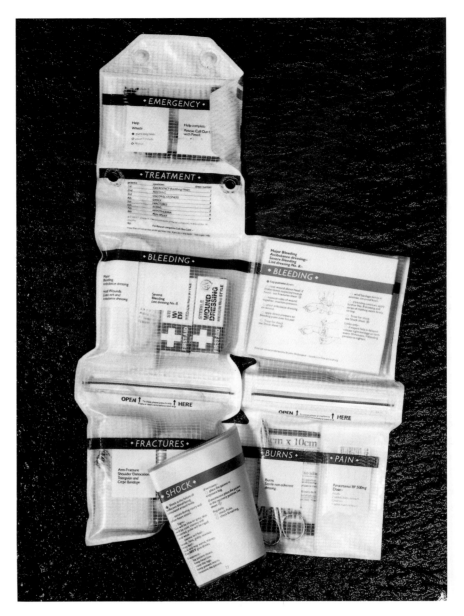

The Gregson first aid pack is one of several available for cyclists.

ness. A few first-aid accessories will take up a tiny space in your luggage, and this is particularly important if you are part of a group which includes inexperienced cyclists. This kit could be simply a small ball of cotton wool (to clean grit or dirt from a graze) and a length of self-adhesive plaster that can be cut to size. A group of cyclists might carry a more extensive first-aid kit.

Bad bruises are best splashed with cool water and may be lightly strapped. If necessary continue thereafter in a low ('high revs') gear, to prevent yourself from stiffening up. A strain should be rested for half an hour with the limb

held up above the heart, with cold water applied. It can then be strapped in a compression bandage before you proceed with caution.

Jim McGurn often takes a small kit of homoeopathic medicines with him. This ancient form of medicine, which is enjoying a resurgence in popularity, involves a range of tablets, each containing a minute quantity of a substance which would in larger doses cause an ailment similar to the one you are seeking to cure. Thus the body is induced to react in such a way that it heals itself. Arnica is therefore excellent for shock or bruising, and can be used in cream form if the skin is not cut – it's often a good remedy for saddle soreness. Other homoeopathic medicines can be used with lasting effect against hay fever, sunburn and most other problems which can come the way of the cyclist. See page 95 for further reading on homoeopathy.

If you get something in your eye which you cannot blink away, avoid rubbing it. Try tipping your head back and pouring clean water from your bottle on to your eye.

If an ache develops in your knee, it is possible that your bike or your pedalling style needs adjustment. Perhaps your saddle is too low and limits the extension of the leg, or you have been pedalling in too high a gear.

Cycling, and especially the long-distance variety, tends to exercise a fairly limited number of muscles and joints. It makes sense to exercise those parts that may ache during or after a long ride, particularly the back and neck. A simple and safe method of stretching your back to relieve aches is to stand with your feet slightly apart, and, with your hands clasped behind your buttocks, lean down from the hips and hold the position for half a minute or more. Try this first with one leg slightly bent and slightly forward of the other to stretch the straight leg. Repeat with the other leg bent, and then try it (gently) with both legs straight.

To stretch both back and neck, stand with your feet apart and your hands on your hips. Turn your trunk and head to look as far as you can to one side and hold that posture. Then do the same exercise looking the other way.

The neck alone can be exercised by gently rolling your head, ear to shoulder, chin to chest, other ear to other shoulder, and back again. Do this several times in one direction, before doing it again in the reverse direction.

If you have recurring aches and pains which you think are related to your cycling activities, it is probable that your bike is wrongly set up for you. Read Chapter 3 on how to set your bike up for your own needs.

CHAPTER TWELVE

Family Cycling

Most children can use a childseat from around eight months onwards. Choose a seat to suit the age of your child, and go for quality.

Opposite You can use all kinds of pedal powered vehicle for light off-road rides. There can be a problem getting them over some access restrictions put in place to keep motor bikers off designated cycle paths.

Families, and especially children, can have more fun and independence by cycling off-road, away from the streets tyrannised by motor traffic. Like any other cyclist, however, a child's enjoyment will depend to a large extent on having the right machine. Even the fittest children can be exhausted by a longish recreational ride on a small, single-speed bike with duff bearings.

Good quality, however, costs – which can come as a shock to parents who expect the price of a child's bike to be proportional to the size of the machine. They can have just as many parts, and require the same careful assembly as adult bikes. There are, of course, some fairly cheap infants' bikes. Here costs are reduced by using nylon bushings instead of ball-bearings. This may be adequate for a toy, but the machine is unlikely to outlast more than two years of hard wear, and will deteriorate very quickly.

Robust children's bikes became widely available with the BMX craze. These bikes can be strong, simple to maintain and perfectly suitable for modest distances. As the child grows the choice widens to scaled-down mountain bikes. You need to consider how much complexity your child can deal with, and whether it would be prudent to opt for a bike with a single chainring. You can also start to encourage your child to take on basic maintenance tasks, starting with pumping up the tyres and lubricating the chain.

Many children will prefer to share the pedalling effort with an adult. A shared machine will also allow an adult to power a weary child home. You can quickly adapt your own machine by attaching a 'trailer bicycle', which can be transferred to other bicycles with appropriate attachments. This is a cheaper and more adaptable alternative to a full-blown tandem designed for an adult at the front and a child at the rear. As trailer bicycles are not yet very common, they have a good resale value, provided they are maintained in good condition. Trailer bikes are suitable for five- to ten-year-olds or children up to about six and a half stone. A small child will relish the progression from the passivity of a child seat and make a genuine contribution to the pedalling effort. Generally they have small wheels with a single speed, but more sophisticated models can be custom built with full size wheels and derailleur gears.

If all the family enjoys cycling, a tandem will be an excellent investment.

A sturdy trailer for carrying one or two children. For well-surfaced off-road use only.

They can take a child seat and tow trailers. An increasing number of off-road tandems are now available. Many off-the-shelf tandems are low enough at the rear to accommodate children from approximately eight years old. Any standard tandem can be adapted by the substitution of a smaller saddle and the addition of kiddy-cranks, crank shorteners or pedal blocks. You may also need child-safety bars to prevent the child slipping off. Kiddy-cranks are a small pair of cranks which clamp on to the tandem's rear seat tube about ten inches above the normal pedal position, and a chain links them to a freewheel sprocket of the same size at the tandem's bottom bracket. Crank shorteners make tandem cranks suitable for shorter legs. They are basically steel adapters which screw into the pedal hole; the pedal then fits into the inner end of the shortener about 3.5cm further up the crank. Pedal blocks fit either side of a pedal platform, and make the pedal thicker by about an inch, shortening the reach by that amount. They are easily home-made from blocks of wood, bolted through the pedal.

Most touring tandems will not have the pedal clearances for off-road riding, and even off-road style tandems can cause problems here. The rider on the front can co-ordinate pedalling with the avoidance of protruding tufts of earth and so on. He or she cannot then be aware of where the rear set of

pedals are in relation to an uneven surface, resulting in damage to rear pedals, cranks and bottom bracket.

Trikes can be great fun off-road, but you have to think very hard about what your wheels are doing. Purpose-built child-carrying tricycles are stable and sociable workhorses. Most carry two children in either rear- or forward-facing seats, with space for luggage in the tray below. Taking a shopping trike on gentle but unsurfaced off-road rides is quite an experience. Constant shifts of body weight are needed to cope with sudden sideways lurches.

On a normal bicycle small children can be carried in a child seat fitted on to a rear rack, and these are quite suitable for use on moderately rough tracks, but the rack and fittings must be as sturdy as possible. The child must be able to sit up and hold its head steady (usually by nine months). The upper limit is set by weight: around 20kg. This is because even tiny children affect bike handling as the weight is far above, and perhaps behind, the rear axle.

There are numerous child seats on the market. Choose one which has some support for the child's head – many don't – as even older children may well fall asleep during a ride. Lolling over the side is distressing for children and adversely affects bike handling. Other essential features are: footrests, which should be adjustable and have retaining straps; waist and shoulder straps; and complete spoke and wheel protection. Some seats are designed for younger children, others for older children. One seat in particular deserves a mention. The Roadgear child seat has all the above advantages, and also allows the back of the seat to be tilted rearwards for when the child nods off to sleep. There are few things more difficult to cope with than the feel of a sleepy child's head bouncing against the small of your back as you ride along.

If you have a child on the back, any luggage is best carried in low-rider front panniers for good weight balance.

Consider the following safety matters when carrying children. It is wise to err on the side of caution with all child-carrying devices. Nuts, bolts and stress points should be checked regularly and take care to prevent straps, scarves or gloves on strings from dangling into a wheel. You should also practise on quiet roads when you first try out any child-carrying device, particularly child seats. Remember you are the one doing all the pedalling to keep warm, not your child, so they can easily become cold, and never leave a child unattended in a child seat. Be aware that children can easily become bored on longer journeys, you may need to stop every few miles to let them play. If you carry on regardless they could develop a real antipathy to cycling. Taking along a favourite toy may help. Sprung saddles can also present dangers. Make sure that they are covered properly – probing fingers can often get caught in them.

Cycling together as a family can be a great joy, and off-road riding gives a real sense of shared excitement. It'll mean quite an investment in bikes and equipment, but will open young minds to new experiences and adventures.

Trailer bikes make off-road riding fun for children too big for a childseat, but too young for independent riding.

While you enjoy the exercise a child in a childseat can get bored. It's wise to stop every so often for a little recreation.

CHAPTER THIRTEEN

Cycling and Other Interests

Riding an ancient green road. Cross-country cycling can be a delight for the amateur historian.

Opposite Taking your time means taking in the joys of nature. When you're cycling off-road you can stop any time to appreciate what you see.

'Follow your genius closely enough and it will not fail to show you a fresh prospect every hour,' said Thoreau. You may have gathered by now that our personal style of cross-country cycling is leisurely and meandering. Why rush through beautiful countryside? Some of the loveliest places in Britain are so small and compact that they are worth lingering over and around.

There are all manner of interests and activities which the cross-country cyclist can enjoy instead of simply clocking up the mileage. Away from the monotony of agri-business, and built-up areas, your non-invasive form of transport can bring you in close contact with wildlife in its natural habitat. The rural landscape may also show the signs of long-abandoned activities and ancient highways, giving you insights into local history. The first guide to widening your enjoyment of cycling is an Ordnance Survey map. This will mark the sites of historical buildings, past industry, Roman roads, drover roads and abandoned railways.

One of our favourite cross-country cycling areas is the Yorkshire Dales. We find there a Roman road from Ingleton to the fort at Bainbridge, which marches over the tops at Flett Moss then drops to join the Pennine Way for a while as Cam High Road, and much of this route is cyclable. Monastic settlements determined many routes in both the Yorkshire Dales and the moors, where abbeys such as Rievaulx, Bylands, Jervaulx and Fountains owned large swathes of countryside, and established industries. Many lead mines in the Dales were owned by monasteries, for which packhorse trails were developed because horses could follow tracks across the uplands which would defeat wheeled vehicles. Horses were assembled in trains of twenty to forty with the lead horse having bells on its bridle to keep the rest following. They carried 'wackas' or panniers on each side and could be seen as late at 1870–80 in the Yorkshire moors, where they carried iron and coal.

Packhorse trails were also called 'pannier trods', and were surfaced with flagstones where they traversed boggy moorland surfaces. One such is marked on the OS map as the bridlepath running from Rosedale across the moors to Fryup Dale. Look at this area on the map and you will see evidence of iron workings through the ages, culminating in the building of a railway

which crossed the high moors, at an altitude of over 1000 feet, for a distance of over eleven miles.

To study the historical changes of your area in greater detail, ask at the public library to see the oldest map they have. By 1873 the Ordnance Survey had completely mapped England and Wales, but Scotland took another fifteen years. Reprints of the first series maps can be ordered through bookshops from David and Charles.

Old place-names can give clues to tracing ancient routes and vanished industries. For example, the Old Norse word *wath* (ford) can indicate where a packhorse trail crossed a stream in Yorkshire. Place-names can provide information of archaeological interest with reference to fortifications or burial places. Other names reflect the divisions that used to exist among the social hierarchy. Kington, Athelington, Earlston, Knighton and Carlton illustrate the impact of all ranks of society from those of noble birth to the peasantry. Other names, such as Faulkland, Buckland, Fifehead, Galmpton and Manton, indicate various aspects of land tenure in Anglo-Saxon times. Checking place-names may illuminate the landscape through which you cycle. The Oxford University Press publishes several excellent dictionaries of place-names.

Off-road routes can present you with some unexpected diversions. On the verge of a five-mile stretch of converted railway track, south of York, there are about a dozen apple trees and a single pear tree. We surmised that these grew from cores shied from carriage windows long ago – we may discover some rare old varieties if we study them closely. Last summer, with a friend, we picked several pounds of greengages by the side of a similar track at Hornsea. In summer you can hunt for raspberries, wild strawberries and several edible mushrooms. In autumn you can hunt blackberries, sloes (for gin), mushrooms, elderberries, hips and haws. If you want to partake of this feast remember to pack a suitable container to carry your prizes home. Buy a reference book, such as *Food for Free* by Richard Mabey.

Tracks with mature trees and high hedgerows provide a complete contrast to the surrounding closely managed farmland. The remaining ballast alongside converted railway tracks will quickly become colonised by plants that can survive such poor conditions in contrast to the richer vegetation of the verges. You'll see hares and rabbits pop across, and finches flit along the fences ahead of you.

Once we saw a barn owl flying parallel to us. Indeed cycling and birdwatching go perfectly together. You can patrol tracks inaccessible to motor vehicles, your approach is relatively silent, and you can easily carry a pair of binoculars. Different parts of the country have their characteristic birds, and one particular bird can become emblematic of the area to the cycle tourist. The loud mournful cry of the curlew announces that you are climbing into the Yorkshire Dales and perfectly complements the bleak moor tops. On the Welsh borders the harsher shriek of the buzzard calls from the mixed patchwork of woodland and open ground which it prefers, where you can

A bar bag fitted out with foam protects photographic equipment from damage, and keeps it close to hand.

Above left Biking and birding go together perfectly. The bicycle gives the birdwatcher access to many habitats, without damage or disturbance. *Above* Versatile photographic clamp weighs little and allows a greater variety of photographic techniques.

spot them soaring overhead in huge circles. On a more modest and local scale, bird-watching is an ideal pursuit for the shorter winter rides. The countryside might look dull and dormant, but birds are very active foraging for precious food, and smaller birds are better observed in hedgerows devoid of leaf cover. You may be arrested by the sight of colourful goldfinches working over seedheads. Larger birds like fieldfares, redwings and lapwings feed in flocks in the open fields.

Butterflies are another form of wildlife which flourishes on the varied and open vegetation found beside some tracks. Britain has fifty-seven species of resident native butterflies with a further half a dozen or so visitors from abroad. Very few are as common as they once were, and many species have disappeared from areas where they were once common. Destruction of hedges, the heavy deployment of agrochemicals, and the ploughing up of ancient pastures have all combined to reduce the butterfly population, along with their foodplants. The Butterfly Conservation Society (see p.95) was set up to attempt to curb the decline. They produce a range of booklets, ranging from butterfly identification to hints on photography, which would add further interest to your cycle trips.

Photography is an obvious hobby to combine with cycling. Bar bags and pannier trunk bags will readily accommodate photography equipment, with padding – either supplied by the manufacturers or carved from foam – to cushion your valuable equipment against the shock. You can strap a tripod to the bike, using bungy straps or a compact clamp. We have made one from a spare plastic lamp bracket by fitting a bolt that has the same thread as a tripod screw. This can be clamped to the bike, thus forming a bipod, or to a fence, or to a D lock balanced against a rock. You can get excellent results from a compact 35mm camera with a closing lens cover that will slip into your pocket.

Your bicycle can lead you to activities which are pure fun. A member of our local cycling campaign always carries a kite on coastal rides. It takes up very little space, and can absorb you for hours while you linger at your favourite beauty spot and everyone else lingers over lunch. Kites can be packed into a tube and strapped to the frame, while those without spars can be folded and packed away in your luggage.

CHAPTER FOURTEEN

Camping

For some cyclists true camping has to involve the pleasures of cooking on a lightweight portable stove.

Cycle camping is a wonderfully liberating activity. You can cruise along with everything that you need for travel and accommodation on board with you. Knowing that you could improvise a site inspires a sense of freedom. Your bike might feel as heavy as an oil tanker when you first set off, but you quickly adapt to the changed handling characteristics and a reasonable range of gears will carry you over most hills. It's certainly a lot less cumbersome than carrying everything on your back.

The cyclist is as preoccupied with saving space as the backpacker, so most of the camping equipment available is suitable for both pursuits. The tent should be lightweight and compact enough to fit into your largest pannier. It won't be cheap, since durable, lightweight tents have to be carefully constructed using expensive materials. If you have a touring companion weight and bulk is not so critical because you can share the load: one takes the tent, the other takes most of the other equipment. If you are cycling off-road and camping in exposed places you clearly need a tent that is going to be secure against the wind, and so should have a low profile. This characteristic, together with the requirement for low weight, means that the inner dimensions are likely to be a little cramped. Edgar Newton has a lightweight two-person tent that is fine for solo camping but would require military discipline to accommodate two fully grown people. So consider carefully the dimensions of the tent, rather than just the label, when buying one. Also look at the scope for additional storage of luggage outside the inner tent but protected by the fly sheet.

If you're going to buy a tent it's best to see it when erected. The best place in the world for viewing cyclists' tents is at the Cyclists' Touring Club Rally held in York in early summer each year. A stroll round the campsite will reveal the most popular models and some of the larger camping shops will have a couple of erected tents on display, which will give you an idea how the stated dimensions look in reality.

Lightweight tents come in a number of basic designs. The traditional ridge model will often have a taut ridge between two vertical aluminium poles, one of which may be shorter than the other, to save weight and lower the profile against the wind. This means you can lie only one way round in it.

Opposite The whole hog. This is the kit and the tent taken by two cyclists on a trans-continental cycling tour.

There is little to match the feeling of freedom and independence involved in touring on a bike loaded up with camping gear.

Dome tents have one or two long flexible poles which bend inside a sleeve in the fly sheet to form a dome high enough for a person to sit up in it. They can be very stable in demanding conditions. Tunnel tents have a number of separate hoops which create space well, although they can be more vulnerable in a side wind.

Your sleeping-bag is the other crucial and costly item of equipment. Down-filled bags are highly regarded for their retention of warmth and for folding into a compact parcel. To retain their insulation they require careful cleaning with specialist shampoos that can be purchased at camping shops. Sleeping-bags containing synthetic fibres are easier to clean and dry, but are generally bulkier. Sleeping-bags should conserve your body heat but avoid cold spots. They are quilted to form pockets to hold the filling material in place, and to achieve this cheaper bags may have the inner and outer shells sewn directly together. Insulation will be limited along those lines where both sides meet. This situation is avoided in better quality sleeping-bags by forming adjoining box-shaped compartments, with the vertical walls separating inner and outer shells. Other techniques use slanting walls, or alternating V-shaped tubes of filling laid against each other. There is now such a wide range of specifications and price that it's worth consulting a few specialist outdoor-pursuit catalogues before you buy.

More warmth can be retained in a sleeping-bag by using a special liner designed to conserve heat. You can also lay a thin foam mat underneath the sleeping-bag for greater insulation and comfort. Both these items are fairly light to carry in a stuffsack strapped to the top of the pannier rack.

When camping on your own, you could make do with a little, solid-fuel Esbit stove to brew up an essential cup of tea or coffee. You can pretend to be a real camper by poking little twigs underneath to stoke the fire. You can use a stove like this to warm up a can of something to eat too, but if this is all you have, elaborate cooking is out and a pub supper is probably on the cards. You can increase the scope of your cuisine by taking a meths stove like the Trangia, which is light to carry and packs up with its utensils. These are apparently the Boy Scout's favourite, judging from the range in our local Scout's shop. They are inexpensive at around £30. Meths has the advantage of being widely available in small quantities, and of maintaining its heating properties even in a draught. It has a tendency to seep, so it is best carried in a specially designed fuel bottle with a deep-threaded cap. There are a number of multi-fuel stoves available which are slightly more expensive, as well as numerous gas-cartridge stoves.

An important last consideration for the cycling camper is to keep the feet dry. It is all too easy to get your feet soaked cycling, and then return to a sodden campsite. Flip-flops might be a solution in high summer, but in cooler weather you really need dry footwear to feel warm. A change of socks and shoes or boots will of course add to the weight but might be important to your comfort.

When you are camping with a bicycle you will be making the maximum use of limited luggage space. So, no matter how much you scorn the over-organised holiday-maker, plan and list your equipment in advance, particularly if you are sharing the trip with another person.

Tent design is an advanced science. Look for strength, lightness, packability, breathability and ease of erection.

CHAPTER FIFTEEN

Fitness, Fresh Air and Fun

feeling the benefits

You have now taken your new bike on a few delightful rides and returned feeling refreshed and pleased with yourself, having made such good progress under your own steam. Here are some ideas for increasing your enjoyment.

As we said in Chapter 5, on a bicycle you become the most energy-efficient animal under the sun. The bicycle converts your energy smoothly, making it an excellent machine for exercise because you can gradually build up the work to the energy level you feel you need. Some commonly accepted guidelines on exercise developed by the American Colleges of Sports Medicine state that for exercise to be effective, you should do the following:

* use at least 50–60 per cent of the total possible volume of your oxygen uptake
* make the exercise last for a minimum of twenty minutes
* practise between three and five times a week
* exercise the large muscle groups rhythmically rather than in a spasmodic or jerky way, such as jogging.

Cycling fits this bill perfectly. You don't need special clothes or extra equipment; nor do you need to join a club or even advertise that you're taking exercise. You may only be returning your library books or nipping down to the shops, but if you perhaps choose a circuitous route you can fit in twenty minutes of mild effort.

A key message in a recent report on the National Fitness Survey, published by the Sports Council and the Health Education Authority, is that:

> it doesn't have to hurt to get fit but you do need to get out of breath or build up a sweat. Activity levels need to be sufficient to raise the heart rate to between 60 and 80 per cent of its estimated maximum (220 beats per minute minus a person's age) if fitness and health benefits are to be achieved.

The Department of Transport National Travel Survey 1985–6 found that three-quarters of all journeys are less than 8km (five miles). This is an ideal distance for a regular exercise ride. Look at ways in which you can incorpor-

Opposite It does not have to hurt to get fit, but you do need to get out of breath.

On a bicycle you are the most energy efficient animal under the sun.

ate cycling within your lifestyle and you can save on transport costs and keep fit at the same time. After a while you will discover that your bicycle is quicker than your car for shorter trips, especially in towns and cities.

As cycling is so efficient you will not get much exercise unless you consciously push the pedals briskly. Choose a route that is unbroken by frequent stops (such as traffic lights) and build up your speed until you notice that your breathing is deeper, and you are feeling warmer – you are now exercising aerobically, making your heart and lungs work harder, improving in turn the efficiency of the body's internal system and increasing the amount of oxygen that you can process. If you do this three or four times a week you will notice yourself becoming generally fitter and better able to manage the route with ease. If you want to improve your fitness still further try to fit in some longer rides. Riding regularly for an hour or clocking up about fifteen miles will bring good gains, not only in endurance but basic aerobic capacity as well, if you maintain a brisk pace.

Few cyclists see on- and off-road cycling as alternatives. Rather they are part of a continuum. Riding round town during the week gives one the fitness and riding skills useful for a weekend off-road, and riding across country can be physically demanding compared to travelling on tarmac.

Riding over rough surfaces makes particularly high demands on your energy reserves.

After several weeks' regular cycling you will notice a real improvement in performance. A good sign is when you realise that you have some energy left at the end of a longer ride, allowing you to accelerate with a flourish over the home stretch. During the ride, try cycling almost flat-out for short intervals so that you feel your legs really working and you are breathing hard. Listen to your body and make it work vigorously, but build up to this gradually, so that you will improve your performance without coming to any harm.

We have used subjective criteria for judging fitness, but if you become really keen, there are books on competitive cycling that deal with training in considerable depth. Both professional and amateur racers now take a much more scientific approach to their cycling rather than simply cycling the long distances they did in the past to 'put the miles in their legs'. They have a keen awareness of aerobic and anaerobic thresholds, and are aided by such gadgets as pulse meters. At peak effort, when you are working anaerobically, you draw energy from glycogen stored in the muscle. This creates lactic acid as waste which will eventually build up sufficiently to limit muscle function and cause pain. A professional racer develops a fine awareness of how far he or she can call on such anaerobic reserves for intense

bursts of effort, such as sprints and hill climbs, before the build-up of lactic acid forces him or her to slow down.

Such acute awareness is essential for road racers who hurtle over a hundred miles a day at high speeds in tight groups. The average speed of the 1992 Tour de France was 24.5 mph. In 1990 Gianni Bugno covered the 182 miles of the Milan–San Remo one-day classic at an average speed of 28.463mph. You need to enter this sport young, and train for years, to acquire the skills to keep up with the bunch.

With cross-country cycling you can remain a happy amateur and still enjoy competitive events. You might need to acquire a full-blooded mountain bike to do so. In the heat of competition you are unlikely to think about preserving the bike, so it will come in for a lot of abuse. If you're looking for a more subtle pursuit you could try observed trials, which are a series of short sections over terrain packed with obstacles, each one calling for precise control and balance, and split-second judgment. Competitors approach each section one at a time to negotiate their particular difficulties, ideally without putting a foot down. As the bike has to clear exaggerated obstacles, trial bike riders favour a high bottom bracket, a short wheelbase to manoeuvre in tight spots, and sometimes a high riding position so they have to lean back less to pull the front wheel up. Twenty-inch wheels may be used, which allow an even shorter wheelbase. It is quite easy for a small, informal group of enthusiasts to devise their own course by utilising the existing terrain imaginatively or creating obstacles with blocks, logs and whatever comes to hand.

A new style of cross-country event was launched in 1991 which combines orienteering, riding and basic survival skills. The Polaris Challenge is a two-day orienteering event for off-road cyclists. The terrain includes tarmac, forest tracks and open moorland. Farm gates and trail junctions become checkpoint posts for the weekend. Each post has a point value and a card punch. Teams of two cyclists rush from post to post to amass points and return to base within the allotted time. Each team must carry a tent, food for thirty-six hours, tool kit, stove and cooking equipment, map and first-aid kit. In addition they must have at least one front and one rear light per team for safe riding if caught out at night. Nearly 200 teams take part in the Challenge, in junior, senior and veteran categories. The care with which it is organised indicates how keen mountain bike organisations are to keep environmental impact to a minimum. The mountain bike code has to be observed at all times, and a large wall map shows checkpoints and all the legal riding tracks. Both must be transcribed to the competitors' maps before they can set off on the route they have planned to gain themselves maximum points as well as allowing for a return within the set time.

As part of a developing recreational programme, the British Mountain Bike Federation is developing non-competitive 'festivals' based on general mountain bike matters such as map reading, fun rides and conservation. The opportunities for you to have fun off-road are increasing all the time.

Fully equipped and ready to go. A participant in the annual Polaris Challenge.

CHAPTER SIXTEEN

Invention and Ingenuity

designers of off-road bicycles

Much of the impetus for the mountain bike boom came from America, with design reflecting American needs. However, British designers have been producing strikingly original mounts for as long as the Americans.

Geoff Apps had been preoccupied since 1970 with the notion of combining the thrill and fun of motorcycling off-road with the pleasure, peace and nature-friendliness of cycling. By 1978, after years of searching for suitable hardware, drawing up ideas and walking home because of mechanical failure, his thoughts had developed to the point of submitting an entry for the *Sunday Times* 'Bike of the Future' competition. He distilled his ideas into a drawing and two pages of text, but was astonished at the ineptitude of the judges in their attitude to the 'leisure bicycle': 'the entries included a lot of machines looking much like one-person-powered scramble motor cycles . . . none seemed really inspired'. They had completely missed the point. What Apps was working towards emerged in 1980 as the 'Range Rider', 'the Range Rover of bicycles'.

Geoff Apps on his Clelandale.

The original catalogue of these machines featured a fresh-complexioned young Englishman riding a very upright mount along a stream bed through woods, like a knight in search of the Holy Grail. The details make fascinating reading: 'the bottom bracket axle height is 12⅞ inches. This added height gives an actual ground clearance of 8 inches which allows the use of long cranks for extra torque as well as the ability to jump considerable obstacles *en route*.' A bash plate was fitted around the chainwheel to protect it over obstacles, 'aiding the general operation with a sort of *skating* action. With a little practice you are up, over and away – even a log of 20 inches diameter presents no problem . . . The top tube is lowered to avoid straddling, with a double-taper, duplex triangulating cross brace.'

The tyres were Stud Hakkas, designed for riding in snow and ice, with a deep knobbly offset tread pattern and tiny tungsten carbide studs. To deal with mud, an alloy chainguard was fitted between the rear wheel and the chain, and it had mudguards with clearances of two inches. A twin-coil spring saddle supported an upright riding position. Apps's own hub brakes provided reliable stopping power, even in the rain.

So there you have an entirely British design built to cope with our wet,

muddy conditions. In *Richard's Mountain Bike Book* (see p.95), Nick Crane remarks, 'the combination of tyres with tungsten-steel studs and gears low enough to ride up the bathroom wall, gave the bike enough traction to power it up slimy rock-steps and shale that shattered like flakes of ice. The traction was awesome.'

Unfortunately supplies of components for such a novel machine were anything but predictable and Apps ran out of money in 1984.

The brazing torch for the true British off-road bike has passed to Dave Wrath Sharman, a designer—engineer who had been thinking about designing a 'bridleway bike' for walking his dogs along the bridleways in the part of Surrey where he lived. He wanted a bike that could handle both on-road and off-road conditions with precision and efficiency. As most of his early riding was on a track bike — short, stiff and high — his starting point was quite different from the Americans' with their laid-back originals. Originally he modified a ladies' roadster and then bought an Apps machine. He now specialises in producing highly individual bicycles which he regards as pieces of sculpture for pedalling across the landscape, a reflection of his training as a sculptor. The bicycles are custom made and will cost well above £1000. Because he was dissatisfied with the compromise of fitting highly individualised frames with standardised components he also makes many of his own components. 'If I've instigated anything at all,' he told *New Cyclist Magazine*, 'it's the idea of designing the whole bike with as few compromises as possible. I'm not limited to standard bottom bracket widths, I'm not limited to standard dropouts, I'm not limited to standard brakes or hubs, because I make

An original British cross-country tourer, designed and built by Geoff Apps before the US mountain bike boom.

A cross-country bicycle designed by Geoff Apps for practicality, comfort and all-surface traction. Sadly out of production since 1984.

my own'; and 'I'd like to see frame builders and component manufacturers really answering the questions that need answering, instead of simply making the thing look different for the sake of it, so that the product sells on visual appeal rather than performance.' The machines are so stunningly original that far more people have wanted bikes than he can make. His authority as a designer is such that Sturmey Archer, the world's largest producer of hub brakes, have consulted both him and Geoff Apps on hub-brake design.

Another designer producing machines for a technically sophisticated market, but in factory conditions with an increasing output, is Dr Alex Moulton. He introduced the first small-wheeled bike with suspension in 1962, and it became an outstanding success. He started producing his new generation of AM machines in 1983 from his own factory in Bradford-on-Avon. Alex Moulton has approached bicycle construction with engineering principles, which have been further refined in his latest models. The main frame and forks are built extremely stiffly and then allowed to articulate by a known significant amount. Suspension is now of course the latest obsession for off-road cyclists but Dr Moulton, having a start of more than a quarter of a century, introduced his all-terrain bike in 1988. He designed this to be analogous to the well-known Range Rover in terms of off-road performance, rather than a racing machine. The bright yellow, small-wheeled machine was

Mike Burrows, inventor of the 1992 Olympic 'Superbike' here on his experimental carbon-fibre San Andreas off-road machine. Note the cantilever wheels – with their hubs supported on only one side.

as much coveted for its eye-catching appeal in the city as for its performance off-road.

This was superseded in 1992 by the Moulton All-Purpose Bicycle, which is a co-operative venture involving the cycle manufacturer W. R. Pashley and bringing the price of a Moulton bike down through mass-production techniques. The APB is not really intended for extreme off-road riding. Nevertheless, for serious pootling, it is as good as any.

Mike Burrows is another innovative engineer but one who designs bikes as a hobby. Some hobby: a little carbon-fibre number that he had been refining for years was adopted with devastating effects at the 1992 Olympic Games to carry Chris Boardman to a gold medal for the 4000m pursuit. Its inventor was referred to in the French magazine *Cyclisme*, as '*le concepteur de*

la machine infernale'. Not only has Mike designed the track bike, but his recumbent Human Powered Vehicle has become a classic, and he has also knocked up a roadster and an off-road machine. All his bikes are designed with himself as a rider in mind, and there was no attempt to make them immediately commercial. This has allowed him to go back to first principles and devise novel ways of building bikes. He frequently uses carbon fibre, for utility machines as well as aerodynamic record breakers:

> It's very easy stuff to use: you just carve a piece of Styro foam into the required shape, add an alloy tube or two for the head and seat tubes and wrap the whole lot in epoxy resin-soaked carbon fibre. Then you wrap it up tightly in PVC insulating tape and dry off slowly, using a fan heater. (from *New Cyclist Magazine*)

He has experimented with an off-road bike design, using drum brakes, cantilever-mounted wheels, suspension and a monolithic cruciform structure, which unfortunately developed a mind of its own once it left the tarmac behind. He told *New Cyclist Magazine*, 'It is actually a very good "street machine" which is a new category I have created for failed mountain bikes.' Burrows believes that most bikes will be made of carbon fibre in the future.

Still in her early twenties, Isla Rowntree has already made a name for herself as a bike designer. She was one of the winning women's pair in the

Isla Rowntree's hub geared, hub braked town bike is also ideal for most kinds of light off-road riding. It will suit the rider who wants a single, universally useful bike.

original Polaris Challenge in 1991, described in Chapter 15, and is a top women's mountain bike competitor. She started producing trailer bikes with Andy Thompson in 1990. She feels that the bicycle industry has failed to produce quality utility machines because in Britain, unlike on the Continent, there's a perception of the bike as poor man's transport. She attracted a great deal of attention at the 1992 York Cycle Rally with an eye-catching, hub-geared, hub-braked town bike. She intends to put this into production. It's aimed at commuters and town cyclists but would also be ideal for light off-road use:

> With this bike, I wanted to try to put everything you'd need on the bike before it's sold (racks, mudguards, lights, etc.). I've also used high-quality materials and components. A commuting bike is likely to be used more than any other bike, and therefore needs to be reliable and efficient.
> (from *New Cyclist Magazine*)

These designers show the tremendous amount of ingenuity and innovation which is being expended on bicycle design, and the variety of settings in which this can be conducted, from home workshops to factory. The most significant innovations since the war, such as the small-wheeled bicycle and the carbon-fibre track machine, have been the inspiration of individuals, not large firms. Bicycle technology is human-scale technology and there is no reason why you should not design and perhaps even construct your own bicycle, with a little help, should you feel so inspired.

CHAPTER SEVENTEEN

Information

Ballantine. Richard, *Richard's Bicycle Book*, Pan, 1990. The classic book on the bicycle and an excellent manual for beginners. It covers cycling generally, not just off-road technology.

Bogdanowicz. Tom, et al, *The Off-Road Bicycle Book*, Leading Edge, 1992. Now in its third edition, this is a good introduction to the British scene, with contributions by some intelligent authorities.

Evans. Jeremy, *Off-Road Adventure Cycling*, The Crowcad Press, 1990. Contains fifty routes in England.

Goudie. A, and R Gardener, *Discovering Landscape in England and Wales*, Allen and Unwin, 1985.

Harland. Madaleine, and Glen Finch, *The Barefoot Homeopath: Health Care for the Whole Person*. Available direct from Hyden House Ltd, Little Hyden Lane, Clanfield, Hants, PO8 ORU. A comprehensive self-help guide for minor injuries.

Hoskins. WG, *The Making of the English Landscape*, Hodder and Stoughton, 1992.

Kelly. Charles, and Nick Crane, *Richard's Mountain Bike Book*, Series Ed. Richard Ballantine, Oxford Illustrated Press, 1988.

Mabey. Richard, *Food for Free*, HarperCollins, 1989.

McGurn. James, ed. *Encycleopedia*, Open Road, 4 New Street, York, July 1993. A compendium of little known and specialised cycles and equipment. Only some of the products are appropriate to cross-country cycling.

Mitchell. F, *The Shell Guide to Reading the Irish Landscape*, 1986.

Muir. R, *The Shell Guide to Reading the Landscape*, 1981.

Osbourne. Peter Koch, *The Cairngorm Glens: A guide for walkers and mountain bikers*, Cicerone Press, 1991.

Stevenson. John, *Mountain Bikes, Maintenance and Repairs*, Springfield Books, 1991. This book is packed with excellent photos of young chaps getting their hands authentically greasy and might encourage the youth of the house to take a more than superficial interest in their expensive machines. The large format lies flat when open on workbench or coffee table.

Taylor. C, *Roads and Tracks of Britain*, Dent, 1979.

Wilson. John Graham, *Follow the Map*, Black, 1985.

CTC, *Cycle A-way*, 1992. A useful little booklet containing a concise guide to cycle routes in the British Isles. It lists designated cycle routes in different counties as well as sources of information, which is particularly useful since leaflets are now available from a range of different local authority departments. Forestry and canal trails and commercially produced guides are also listed. You can buy a copy from CTC Shop, Cotterell House, 69 Meadrow, Godalming, Surrey GU7 3HS, price £1.50.

The Isle of Wight has a set of four leaflets on *Byways and Bridleways by mountain bike* from the Isle of Wight County Surveyor's Department, County Hall, Newport, Isle of Wight. You can also get a pack of five leaflets of cycle routes in Gloucestershire, including the Forest of Dean from Gloucestershire Tourism, Planning Department, Shire Hall, Gloucester GL1 2TN. There are similar suggested routes for cyclists appearing in most parts of the country, some of which will contain off-road sections. Do some detective work by contacting the relevant Tourist Office, National Park Information Centre, or the local office of the Forestry Commission.

MAGAZINES

New Cyclist, 67–71 Goswell Road, London EC1V 7EN. A general interest cycling magazine for the intelligent reader. Not primarily an off-road cycling magazine, although off-road matters are regularly covered. Editor in Chief is Jim McGurn.

Mountain Biking UK, Future Publications, 30 Monmouth Street, Bath.

Mountain Biker, Northern and Shell plc, PO Box 381, Mill Harbour, London E14 9TW.

Both mountain bike magazines cater for a youth/fashion market. There is no magazine (as yet) for the more mature off-road rider.

ORGANISATIONS

In many cases a stamped addressed envelope would be appropriate when writing to the following organisations for information.

The **Cyclists' Touring Club** (CTC), Cotterell House, 69 Meadow, Godalming, Surrey GU7 3HS. Tel: 0483 417 217. This is the largest cycling organisation in the country, with 40,000 members. In addition to lobbying for better facilities and access for cyclists, the CTC provides information and advice services on touring, technical, insurance and legal matters. It is primarily a road-touring club, but is taking an increasing interest in off-road activities.

The **British Mountain Biking Federation** (BMBF), 36 Rockingham Road, Kettering, Northants NN16 8HG. Tel: 0536 412211. This organisation administers mountain bike racing and promotes non-competitive off-road riding. It is allied to the British Cycling Federation, a governing body for on-road competition cycling.

The **Rough-Stuff Fellowship** was formed in the 1950s, when the spread of tarmac and cars drew a distinction between cyclists who actively sought off-road routes and those who didn't. The national organisation is divided into areas, and some are more sympathetic to newcomers, with sedate rides organised monthly. The Fellowship's magazine, *The Rough-Stuff Journal*, contains information of interest to the non-competitive cross-country cyclist. Contact: AJ Matthews, 9 Liverpool Avenue, Ainsdale, Southport, Lancs. PR8 3NE. Tel: 0873 880384.

Sustrans, 35 King Street, Bristol BS1 4DZ. Tel: 0272 268893. A registered charity which promotes, designs and builds safe cycle paths, often over long distances.

OTHER INTERESTS

The **Countryside Commission**, John Dower House, Crescent Place, Cheltenham, Gloucestershire GL50 3RA. Tel: 0242 521381. Works to conserve the natural beauty of the English countryside and to help people enjoy it. They publish a variety of leaflets, booklets, reports, guides, and periodicals on countryside conservation, recreation and how to improve access.

Since 1991, the Countryside Commission's responsibilities in Wales have been taken up by the **Countryside Council for Wales**, Plas Penrhos, Ffordd Penros, Bangor, Gwynedd LL57 2LQ. Tel: 0248 370444.

The **British Trust for Conservation Volunteers**, 36 St Mary's Street, Wallingford, Oxon OX10 0EU. Tel: 0491 39766. Active in both conservation and in teaching skills to volunteers. Tasks include improving access through rights of way.

The **Royal Society For Nature Conservation**, The Green, Witham Park, Waterside South, Lincoln LN5 7JR. Tel: 0522 544400. The RSNC represents forty-seven local Wildlife Trusts and fifty urban Wildlife Groups.

The **Butterfly Conservation Society**, PO Box 222, Dedham, Colchester, Essex CO7 6EY. Tel: 0206 322342.

CYCLE HOLIDAYS AND EVENTS

Excellent cycling holidays in Holland (where riding can be almost all off-road) are organised by **Anglo-Dutch Holidays**, 30a Foxgrove Road, Beckenham, Kent BR3 2BD. They also offer cycle tours down the cycle paths along the river Danube.

Off-road riding also forms part of the package offered by **Cobblestone Cycling Holidays** in the Scottish Borders. Contact Jason Patient, Cobblestone Cycling Holidays, 1 Church Lane, Coldstream, Berwickshire, Scotland TD12 4DG. Tel: 0890 88 3408.

Other holiday organisers offer entirely off-road cycling holidays, but check that they are really your cup of tea before booking. Some plug into the mountain bike youth culture; others are fine for almost anybody. Scan the advertisements in cycle magazines early in the year to keep up with what's on offer.

Bike 1 normally specialise in day rides along country lanes, but, beginning in June 1993, they are organising an annual charity ride for Sustrans. This will be taking in some of the long-distance Sustrans cycle paths around York, and takes place on the same weekend as the Cyclists' Touring Club Rally in York. Details from Simon Shaw and Anna Pond, Bike 1 Bicycle Tours, 16 Waterside Court, Old Cove Road, Fleet, Hampshire GU13 8RH. Tel: 0252 624022.